Thomas Cook **pocket** guides

LIVERPOOL

Thomas Cook

Written and updated by David Cawley

Published by Thomas Cook Publishing
A division of Thomas Cook Tour Operations Limited
Company registration no. 3772199 England
The Thomas Cook Business Park, Unit 9, Coningsby Road,
Peterborough PE3 8SB, United Kingdom
Email: books@thomascook.com, Tel: +44 (0) 1733 416477
www.thomascookpublishing.com

Produced by Cambridge Publishing Management Limited
Burr Elm Court, Main Street, Caldecote CB23 7NU
www.cambridgepm.co.uk

ISBN: 978-1-84848-372-9

First edition © 2009 Thomas Cook Publishing
This second edition © 2011
Text © Thomas Cook Publishing
Maps © Thomas Cook Publishing/PCGraphics (UK) Limited
Contains Ordnance Survey data © Crown copyright and database right 2010
Transport map © Communicarta Limited

Series Editor: Karen Beaulah
Production/DTP: Steven Collins

Printed and bound in Spain by GraphyCems

Cover photography © Ludovic MAISANT

CONTENTS

SYMBOLS KEY

The following symbols are used throughout this book:

ⓐ address ⓣ telephone ⓦ website address ⓔ email
ⓛ opening times ⓝ public transport ⓘ important

The following symbols are used on the maps:

i information office		▪ point of interest	
✈ airport		○ city	
✚ hospital		○ large town	
◉ police station		○ small town	
▣ bus station		= motorway	
⊒ railway station		— main road	
✝ cathedral		— minor road	
❶ numbers denote featured cafés, restaurants & venues		— railway	

Hotels and restaurants are graded by approximate price as follows:
£ budget price ££ mid-range price £££ expensive

▶ *The Three Graces with the Museum of Liverpool in the foreground*

INTRODUCING
Liverpool

Introduction

Everybody thinks they know Liverpool, even if they've never visited – The Beatles, football and the chirpy Scouser. Those are the clichés. But there is so much more to this city.

Recently it has been on the up and up in every sense as it has sped through one of the most dynamic and prosperous periods in its history. Regeneration is everywhere: droves of hard-hatted workers clamber up and down endless nests of scaffolding that seem to propel the skyline ever upwards. Historic warehouses and office buildings are metamorphosing into bars and clubs. Indeed, clubs and bars are a speciality here: this is a city that really does know how to enjoy itself. Students from two universities and a number of specialist colleges combine with a very special local lust for life to create a vivacious party atmosphere that really gets into gear when the sun goes down.

Yet by day Liverpool has a calm and cultured feel. It possesses more museums and art galleries than any other English city except London. Art and culture in all their forms – writing, television, architecture, film, painting, music and sport – have a long and illustrious past and a spectacularly bright future here.

High-class retail centres attract shoppers into the central area of town, while along the pedestrianised Lord, Church and Bold Streets, the recently opened Liverpool ONE retail complex and the independent and brand-name stores vie with one another for intimate knowledge of your chip and PIN. When it comes to eating out, Liverpool can compete with anywhere in Europe.

If the urban buzz all becomes too much, rural relaxation in the splendour of the Ribble Valley is close at hand. Or, if some fun beside the seaside is in order, the unspoilt beaches of the Wirral are just a short journey across the River Mersey.

🔺 *Liverpool's marina shows its new-found prosperity*

When to go

As a major commercial and cultural centre, Liverpool is open year-round to visitors, though certain attractions may offer slightly reduced timetables and opening hours during the autumn and winter months. Throughout the summer, the city takes advantage of the weather and plays host to a number of annual festivals. For the rest of the year, sport comes into its own.

SEASONS & CLIMATE

As you find with any UK destination, Liverpool's weather is consistently inconsistent. Visitors can wake up to driving rain and black clouds that quickly clear to reveal pristine blue skies and golden sunshine. This can also work the other way. The best advice is to take clothing for any climatic eventuality. The average January temperature is 4°C (39°F), and although snow is rarely an issue, a bitter northerly wind can come howling up the Mersey from the Irish Sea and cause quite a ruffle. The average temperature in July is 16°C (61°F). While hardly Mediterranean, this makes for comfortable conditions in which to explore the city.

ANNUAL EVENTS
January & February
Chinese New Year As home to one of the oldest Chinese communities in Europe, Liverpool celebrates New Year at the Chinese Arch on Nelson Street with dancing dragons, unicorns and lions, special firecracker performances and t'ai chi demonstrations. Ⓦ www.lcba.net

April

Grand National One of the biggest and most eagerly anticipated horse races in the world takes place in the northern suburb of Aintree. Far from being just a sporting event, the National has become a firm fixture in the social calendar, with many of the spectators getting almost as much attention for their interpretations of fashion as the race. ⓐ Aintree Racecourse, Ormskirk Rd, Aintree ⓣ (0151) 523 2600 ⓦ www.aintree.co.uk

⬤ *The Grand National steeplechase at Aintree*

May & June

Liverpool Comedy Festival Renowned for its local comedic output, Liverpool stages a month-long chucklefest that attracts masters of the art from around the world to perform in venues across the city and Merseyside. Ⓦ www.liverpoolcomedyfestival.co.uk

Liverpool International Tennis Tournament The top players of the moment join legends of the game for some high-quality tennis in the middle weekend of the month. Ⓐ Caulderstones Park, Allerton Ⓣ 0844 847 2332 (Ticketmaster) Ⓦ www.liverpooltennis.co.uk

Africa Oyé The third weekend of the month sees the biggest free African music and cultural festival in the UK taking place in the leafy finery of Sefton Park. Ⓦ www.africaoye.com Ⓔ info@africaoye.com

July

Liverpool Summer Pops Offering a month of big-name stars in the worlds of rock, pop, jazz and folk, the Pops attracts huge audiences to its riverside venue. Artists who have appeared previously include Bob Dylan, Paul Simon, Elton John and Eric Clapton. Ⓐ Liverpool Echo Arena, Monarchs Quay Ⓣ 0844 800 0400 Ⓦ www.echoarena.com

August

Creamfields Clubbers from up and down the country head to a disused airfield on the edge of the city (see website for exact location) for a weekend of dance music and festival shenanigans. Ⓣ (0151) 707 1309 Ⓦ www.creamfields.com

November

Homotopia Liverpool's celebration of gay culture features music, art, cinema and luxurious helpings of fabulous raconteurism. ☏ (0151) 702 7569 ⓦ www.homotopia.net

International Guitar Festival of Great Britain (mid-month) Strummers, pickers and talented pluckers from around the world bring heavy fretting to a variety of venues throughout the Wirral. ☏ (0151) 666 0000 ⓦ www.bestguitarfest.com

PUBLIC HOLIDAYS
New Year's Day 3 Jan 2011; 2 Jan 2012; 1 Jan 2013
Good Friday 22 Apr 2011; 6 Apr 2012; 29 Mar 2013
Easter Monday 25 Apr 2011; 9 Apr 2012; 1 Apr 2013
May Day 2 May 2011; 7 May 2012; 6 May 2013
Spring Bank Holiday 30 May 2011; 28 May 2012; 27 May 2013
Summer Bank Holiday 29 Aug 2011; 27 Aug 2012; 26 Aug 2013
Christmas Day 25 Dec
Boxing Day 26 Dec

Should Christmas, Boxing or New Year's Day fall on a Saturday or Sunday, the Monday – and sometimes the Tuesday – becomes a public holiday.

The sound of the Mersey

Play word association with most people, and the name 'Liverpool' will inspire the instant response: 'Beatles'. This is understandable: the group was the most influential cultural phenomenon of the second half of the 20th century. The city has certainly not been shy about exploiting this heritage, with Beatles shops (see page 80), Beatles tours (see page 53), a Beatles museum (see page 65) and more Beatles tribute acts than you can shake a drum stick at. However, some now think the band's legacy distracts too much attention from the city's other musical talents, and it's undeniable that countless other local bands have made a huge impact on music in the four decades since the Fab Four last played together live.

The big post-Beatles bang came with the opening of Eric's on Mathew Street in 1976. The club brought punk and new wave acts to the city, inspiring Pete Wylie, Julian Cope and Ian McCulloch to form Wah!, The Teardrop Explodes and Echo & the Bunnymen. In the late 1970s, Deaf School begat Big in Japan, who in turn produced Frankie Goes to Hollywood. Then, during the 1990s, the Liverpool-based dance music collective Cream became a worldwide phenomenon.

Today, the ace-bands-per-square-mile ratio remains astonishing. Outfits such as The Coral, The Zutons and The Wombats have all made huge names for themselves – and let us not forget the mighty Atomic Kitten. Even newer groups such as Hot Club (de Paris), SSS and Elle S'appelle continue to fly the Liver flag. The city's musical focal point has now shifted south from Mathew Street to a trio of warehouse-lined streets – Wood,

Fleet and Seel. These are where clubs such as The Krazy House (see page 88), Zanzibar (see page 89) and particularly Korova (see page 88) showcase new talent and play host to established indie acts. Surely some day soon Julian Cope – now a respected antiquarian – is going to discover that this city is built on a very vibey ley line.

⬤ *The Beatles' story is just a part of Liverpool's musical heritage*

History

Formed around a pool on the banks of the River Mersey, 'lifr pol' (as it began life) was for a long time little more than an insignificant fishing hamlet and river crossing point. Then, in 1207, King John propelled it into the big time by making it an official port. Subsequent centuries saw steady expansion in local farming and fishing and then trade in wine from France and skins and hides from Ireland.

During the 16th and 17th centuries, the port became a prosperous conduit for manufacturing industries exporting their goods to America and the West Indies. On visiting the town, the 17th-century writer Celia Fiennes described it as 'a very rich trading town... the houses are of brick and stone, built high and... look very handsome. There is an abundance of persons who are well dressed and fashionable. The streets are fair and long. It's London in miniature as much as I ever saw anything.'

From about 1730, the merchants of Liverpool made huge profits from the slave trade. This was part of a triangular commercial model that saw goods from northern England sold to Africans in return for slaves, who were transported across the Atlantic to the West Indies. From there sugar was brought back to Liverpool in the empty ships. At the end of the 18th century, the actor Charles Macklin was booed in a city theatre for telling the audience that every brick of their town was 'cemented with the blood of an African'.

The mid-19th to early 20th-century period was Liverpool's economic time in the sun. The city attracted large numbers of immigrants, grand buildings were constructed and the docks were at their peak in terms of trade and passengers.

Things began to sour during the 1970s, however, and Liverpool, like the rest of Great Britain, suffered economic recession. The city's reliance on trade and manufacturing meant it was particularly hard hit, and Liverpool became a byword for deprivation and social unrest during the 1980s. Its economy and profile were partly kept afloat by its vibrant music scene and the arrival of the Tate and the Albert Dock development.

Happily, by the time Liverpool celebrated its 800th birthday in 2007, it was back in business, preparing for its renaissance as Europe's Capital of Culture for 2008, which attracted an even wider international audience to witness its already thriving and burgeoning arts and cultural scene. Despite the recent economic downturn, Liverpool continues to be one of the most identifiable, historic and coolest cities in Europe.

◯ *The city's imposing Town Hall*

Lifestyle

No other city population in the UK can claim to have such an identifiably energetic and distinctive character as that of Liverpudlians.

Perhaps it's because the city looks away from the British mainland towards the sea that an attitude of free-spiritedness and independence from the rest of the UK has been created within the people of Liverpool. They certainly exhibit a passionate

● *A civilised pint is a local lifestyle adornment*

sense of home pride. There is also perhaps a certain worldliness gained from the long tradition of overseas contact; indeed, the city now boasts traces of some 60 different tongues in its vocabulary and has among the oldest African and Chinese communities in Europe. The local accent (known as 'Scouse') is largely a fast-talking mishmash of dialects brought in by immigrants. Its name is thought to derive from 'lobscouse', a basic and hearty Scandinavian stew made with lamb and root vegetables.

The local lifestyle and its practitioners have sometimes both been subjected to extreme caricature. In the 1970s and '80s, when the city was at the deepest trough of its economic decline and the population was in mass exodus, the Scouser became synonymous with a type of moustachioed, workshy braggart who complemented his mullet bouffant with sportswear. Such characters, whose real-life inspirations certainly made up a modest proportion of the local population – as their cousins did all around the country – were known locally as 'scallies'.

That stereotype has now largely dissolved. The modern Liverpudlian is an ambitious creature who works hard and plays hard: the end of most working days sees the city animated by the gregarious bonhomie of Scousers out for a good time. Recent housing developments and the economic boom of the early 21st century have been drawing people back to the city centre to live in trendy apartments, and achievement is no longer measured in tonnage of sweets lifted from the pick 'n' mix counter; tofu recipes mastered would be more like it. And, happily in these days of homogeneity, it now seems that youngsters are speaking with a Scouse accent that's congealed to even thicker clots of impenetrability.

Culture

Liverpool is one of the foremost cultural centres in the United Kingdom, with a fine and long tradition of producing and hosting the best in theatre, music and dance. While the range of theatres catering to all tastes is very impressive for a city of Liverpool's size, the number of art galleries is actually the largest in England outside the capital. These display impressive permanent collections and a constant stream of visiting contemporary and traditional exhibitions throughout the year.

The pool of Liverpudlian literary talent is far from shallow. Many poets and writers hail from the city and champion it as an inspiration for their work. The list is huge and includes Beryl Bainbridge, Clive Barker, Alan Bleasedale, Adrian Henri, Carla Lane, Roger McGough, Brian Patten, Lynda La Plante, Phil Redmond, Willy Russell and Alexei Sayle.

The architecture of the city is glorious, particularly that of the docklands and the Pier Head (which was given World Heritage status in recognition of its importance in maritime history). Indeed, Liverpool is home to 2,400 listed buildings.

After London, this is the UK's most filmed city, with directors capitalising on an urban versatility that can double up for the back-alley fire escapes of Manhattan or the cobbled streets of Victorian London. Films shot against Liverpool's landscapes include *Nowhere Boy*, *51st State*, *Letter to Brezhnev*, *Millions*, *Educating Rita*, *Gumshoe* and Guy Ritchie's *Sherlock Holmes*.

The all-important musical tradition here stretches back hundreds of years to both the arrival of overseas visitors from Africa and China and the raucous sea shanties brought back by

○ *The Philharmonic Hall, home to the Royal Liverpool Philharmonic Orchestra*

travelling mariners. Complementing the abundance of magnificent pop groups (see page 12), the Royal Liverpool Philharmonic Orchestra (see page 104) has a long and illustrious history of classical and contemporary performance and is regarded as one of the world's greatest orchestras.

In 2008 this fascinating and heterogeneous heritage was recognised when Liverpool played host to millions of visitors as an official European Capital of Culture. The city has arrived on the world stage.

For up-to-the-minute guides to what's taking place during your visit either go to Ⓦ www.liverpool.com or call in at a tourist information centre for information and advice from the helpful staff (see page 134). They will also be able to point you in the direction of the city's tourist card – live'smart (see page 44).

● *The city's docks reflected in the water*

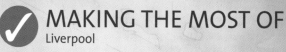

MAKING THE MOST OF
Liverpool

Shopping

Dressing up and going out is a major part of many people's lifestyles here, so it's no surprise that fashion clothing stores have a presence in the local retail experience. Many of the boutiques are exclusive to the city and it's often been suggested that styles in Britain make their first appearance on the streets of Liverpool before filtering out to the rest of the country. For the best shopping in designer labels, Cavern Walks (see pages 74 & 82), the Met Quarter (see page 82) and the Albert Dock (see page 58) are the places to head with a full wallet, while anyone looking for something a bit edgier should head for Grand Central (see page 82) or Bold Street. Those who prefer high-street styles and a less challenging price tag, or are in need of day-to-day items such as toiletries and groceries, should make for Lord Street, Church Street, Clayton Square and **St John's Shopping Centre** (ⓐ 125 St George's Way ⓣ (0151) 709 0916 ⓦ www.stjohns-shopping.co.uk). The latter also has an indoor market, which is not only great for bargains but is also a good source for quality meat, fish and vegetable produce for anyone who is self-catering.

For music lovers there are a number of both national and independent stores throughout the city. Many can be found on Bold Street and the streets running off it, while of course on Mathew Street, The Beatles and their music dominate the retail landscape (see page 78).

Liverpool ONE (ⓦ www.liverpool-one.com), which opened close to the Waterfront in 2008, is a 30-building development the size of 28 football pitches that houses not only a number of large chain stores, an Odeon cinema (see page 31) and choice of restaurants but also the world's largest football club store, which sells anything and everything to do with Liverpool FC.

Most of the city's main shopping streets are now pedestrianised, which makes getting around easy, though it should be noted that between 11.00 and 16.00 on Saturdays they do get extremely busy.

🔺 *Liverpool has no shortage of designer outlets*

Eating & drinking

Whether it be classic British traditional, fashionable fusion, molecular gastronomy, hearty pub grub, international delis or fast-food takeaways, Liverpool has all the cuisine bases covered. The Albert Dock (see page 58) houses a number of trendy eateries and bars, though its popularity among tourists has sometimes led to slightly inflated prices. The Central district and Georgian Quarter offer a good mix of dining experiences, and it's no surprise that the city's long heritage of international trade has played a big part in shaping the eating culture here. The trite 'World in One City' marketing tag that's used to promote tourism is actually quite plausible when applied to eating out. There is an array of international establishments run by people from the countries whose cuisines they represent. Chinatown, which lies on the southern edge of the city centre, offers a particularly fine range of dining (and indeed shopping) experiences.

Along the main commercial thoroughfares and inside the shopping malls, chain restaurants are plentiful. Although they're of limited gastronomic interest, they do offer quick sustenance

PRICE CATEGORIES

The following categorisation represents a guide to average prices per head for a two- or three-course dinner excluding drinks. Lunches are generally cheaper and many places will offer special price incentives for a fixed menu.

£ up to £20   ££ £20–30   £££ over £30

EATING & DRINKING

◐ *Chinatown adds spice to the eating-out profile*

for those with a heavy shopping and sightseeing agenda. The St John's Shopping Centre has a huge choice of fast-food outlets within its lower floor food court. The Liverpool ONE complex even includes a park should the weather suit a picnic, while the benches along the Waterfront around the Pier Head offer a good spot to sit and watch the river traffic. There is a plethora of chain bakeries, supermarkets and delis from which to collect the necessary ingredients for a picnic. Away from the city centre, **Lark Lane** (ⓦ www.larklane.com) possesses a relaxed vibe created by the large student and bohemian population around Sefton Park and a number of good restaurants and bars along its leafy route. Vegetarians are well catered for in this city, especially by the multitude of Eastern and Asian establishments.

When it comes to quaffing options, there are a number of fine, traditional pubs in which you can sample local and international beers. For cocktails and imported beers from around the world, there are swish, fashionable bars scattered throughout the city centre. The strong Irish connection (Liverpool is often jokingly referred to as Ireland's most easterly city) makes for some great traditional evenings, with the 'black stuff' flowing in the many Irish bars.

Gratuity etiquette varies from place to place. Anyone simply having a drink in a traditional pub or bar is not expected to tip; drinks should be ordered and paid for at the bar. If food is served, this too will generally be ordered from the bar and then delivered to your table by a member of staff (a tip might then be appropriate). Restaurants vary in their policy regarding service charges: some may add it to the final bill, while others leave it to the discretion of the customer. If the latter is the case, the general rule is to tip

10 to 15 per cent of the bill. It's advisable to check which option the establishment has gone for to avoid tipping twice.

All public areas, including pubs, bars and restaurants, are strictly non-smoking, though those with space to do so provide patios, terraces and gardens (some heated) to accommodate the smoking community.

⬥ Traditional pubs dot the city's streets

Entertainment & nightlife

Going out and having a laugh is a passion for the people of Liverpool. Whatever the time of year, come the weekend, the streets are thronged with gaily clad *bons vivants* drinking, dancing and looking for romance into the early hours of the morning. The central area of the city can be particularly fun, loud and brash. It can also be hectic and sometimes even a little rowdy – but generally its atmosphere is good-natured and the police make sure things never get overheated. Liverpudlians' predilection for taking pains over their appearance is just as well since many of the bars and clubs have dress policies that are strictly enforced. (This is worth bearing in mind when packing for your visit to Liverpool – sports shoes are especially frowned upon in many venues.)

The area around Concert Square (see page 88) offers the liveliest scene, with a host of R'n'B dance bars and clubs competing for custom with cheap drinks offers. Mathew Street in the Cavern Quarter (see page 78) can have a similar atmosphere, though the numbers of slightly older tourists may create a somewhat retro ambience. The bar and club music here tends to be of a more 1970s, '80s and '90s vintage.

For those who prefer something a little more laid-back (and even slightly more refined), the Georgian Quarter (see page 90) offers a selection of pubs and bars to relax in over a drink before hitting the main concentration of louder late-night venues some ten-minutes' walk away. During academic term time (September to June), the large student population adds to the Quarter's vibrancy, though it certainly never feels too busy.

⬥ *The Liverpool Wall of Fame on Mathew Street*

The Albert Dock (see page 58) is the place to head for celeb-spotting (especially footballing ones). Its collection of chi-chi bars feature minimalist furnishings and loud dance, Latin and R'n'B music that inspires the glitterati to let rip on the dance floors. This area is also home to some of the city's major comedy nights and occasionally hosts live music acts.

While there is as yet no distinctive gay district, Stanley, Dale and Cumberland Streets in the central area all have a number

◓ *The funky interior of the FACT cinema*

WHAT'S ON?

Lifestyle magazine (www.lifestylemonthly.co.uk) is a free monthly glossy featuring interviews and articles and is available from bars, restaurants and newsagents all around the city.

The *Liverpool Daily Post* (www.liverpooldailypost. co.uk) and *Liverpool Echo* (www.liverpoolecho.co.uk) are daily newspapers and contain events listings. Both can be bought from street vendors and newsagents.

of gay, lesbian and bi pubs, clubs and bars that cater for most tastes. Visit www.gayliverpool.com for in-depth information on the budding scene.

There are plenty of live music venues in the city that feature guest DJs and bands. Lovers of the stadium gig need look no further than the **Echo Arena Liverpool** (Monarchs Quay 0844 8000 400 www.accliverpool.com).

The **Odeon** group of cinemas has a number of theatres across Merseyside, including one in Liverpool ONE centre (14 Paradise St 0871 224 4007 www.odeon.co.uk). FACT (see page 79) screens a good selection of blockbuster offerings and the Philharmonic Hall (see page 104) will occasionally offer one-off classic film showings.

If chancing an arm on the tables is your thing, Liverpool has a number of casinos that stay open throughout the night. Putative James Bonds and Pussy Galores should visit www.stanleycasinos.com or www.galacasino.co.uk for details on downtown locations.

Sport & relaxation

SPECTATOR SPORTS

Sport occupies sacred ground in the hearts and minds of Liverpudlians. Golf, horse racing and rugby league draw huge crowds. But football is the predominant spectator sport, and the two principal teams, Liverpool FC and Everton FC, attract a great deal of support locally, nationally and across the world. There is also a third club across the river, Tranmere Rovers, which, while never reaching the giddy heights of its neighbours, still attracts a passionate crowd. Anyone who wants to get a taste of English football and likes to support the underdog would be well advised to take a glimpse at Tranmere, especially since getting tickets for the big boys is far from easy.

Football
Everton Football Club See website for tour details.
ⓐ Goodison Park ⓣ 0871 663 1878 ⓦ www.evertonfc.com
Liverpool Football Club See website for tour details.
ⓐ Anfield Rd ⓣ 0844 844 0844 ⓦ www.liverpoolfc.tv
Tranmere Rovers Football Club ⓐ Prenton Park, Birkenhead
ⓣ 0871 221 2001 ⓦ www.tranmererovers.co.uk

Horse racing
Aintree Racecourse Home of the world-famous Grand National (see page 9). ⓐ Ormskirk Rd ⓣ (0151) 523 2600
ⓦ www.aintree.co.uk
Haydock Park ⓐ Newton-le-Willows ⓣ (01942) 725963
ⓦ www.haydock-park.co.uk

Rugby league
St Helens ⓐ Dunriding Lane, St Helens ⓣ (01744) 455050
ⓦ www.saintsrlfc.com
Widnes Vikings ⓐ Stobart Stadium ⓣ (0151) 495 2250
ⓦ www.widnesvikings.co.uk

PARTICIPATION SPORTS
Golf
Liverpool is at the heart of a golfing region that includes the highest concentration of championship links courses in the world and three famous royal courses:
Royal Birkdale Golf Club ⓐ Waterloo Rd, Southport
ⓣ (01704) 552020 ⓦ www.royalbirkdale.com
Royal Liverpool ⓐ 30 Meols Drive, Hoylake, Wirral
ⓣ (0151) 632 7772 ⓦ www.royal-liverpool-golf.com
Royal Lytham & St Annes ⓐ Links Gate, Lytham St Annes
ⓣ (01253) 724206 ⓦ www.royallytham.org

RELAXATION
Parks
Sefton Park is a large, recently refurbished Victorian park featuring a palm house (see page 44), lakes and mature trees, all surrounded by some of the city's grandest homes and hippest hangouts. In the city centre there are a number of green spaces that make for ideal picnicking areas or rest stops during a hectic schedule, including Falkner Square and Chavasse Park.

Accommodation

Recent years have seen a plethora of new accommodation choices springing up in the city and there should now be something to suit all tastes, including an increasing number of budget and boutique options. While it's always advisable to book in advance, rooms can still be had during the week, particularly in autumn and winter, when the events calendar is at its quietest.

HOTELS

Aachen Hotel £ Close to both the Georgian Quarter and main shopping areas and within easy access of both the rail and coach stations. All-you-can-eat breakfast and a late bar add to the budget appeal of this small, family-run hotel. ⓐ 89–91 Mount Pleasant (The Georgian Quarter) ⓣ (0151) 709 3477 ⓦ www.aachenhotel.co.uk

Beech Mount £ Renovated Grade II listed building consisting of four grand Victorian villas offering 30 rooms in the eastern suburbs of the city. ⓐ 1–4 Beech Mount (The Georgian Quarter) ⓣ (0151) 264 9189 ⓦ www.beechmountexecutive.co.uk

PRICE CATEGORIES
The ratings below indicate average price rates for a double room on a per-night basis, though prices can vary, depending on availability, day of week and season.
£ up to £60   **££** £60–150   **£££** over £150

⬥ *The luxurious Kop Suite at the chic Malmaison*

Dolby Hotel £ Excellent-value modern hotel with many of the facilities you'd expect from a higher price bracket, and well positioned for Waterfront attractions. ⓐ Queen's Dock (The Waterfront) ⓣ (0151) 708 7272 ⓦ www.dolbyhotels.co.uk

Park Lane Hotel £ Built in 1887, this characterful hotel close to Sefton Park offers well-equipped rooms and is 3.2 km (2 miles) from the centre. ⓐ 23 Aigburth Drive, Sefton Park (The Georgian Quarter) ⓣ (0151) 727 4754 ⓦ www.theparklanehotel.co.uk

● *Cool, crisp comfort at the Hope Street Hotel*

62 Castle Street ££ Swish boutique hotel in the heart of the business district, yet only moments away from everything the city centre has to offer. The rooms are packed with gadgets among cool contemporary furnishings. An affordable indulgence. ⓐ 62 Castle St (Central Liverpool) ⓣ (0151) 702 7898 ⓦ www.62castlest.com

Britannia Adelphi Hotel ££ While this monolithic hotel has lost much of its elegance, there are still plenty of original features to marvel at (see page 84). ⓐ Ranelagh Place (Central Liverpool) ⓣ (0151) 709 7200 ⓦ www.adelphi-hotel.co.uk

Epstein House ££ Former home of The Beatles' manager, Brian Epstein, this privately run nine-bedroom guesthouse is located in the suburbs close to both Liverpool and Everton football grounds and, unsurprisingly, features showbiz memorabilia. ⓐ 27 Anfield Rd ⓣ 07932 450 450 ⓦ www.brianepsteinhotel.com

Express By Holiday Inn ££ Modern and comfortable hotel creatively integrated into the former warehouse complex at the heart of the Albert Dock and just a short stroll from many of the tourist attractions. ⓐ Albert Dock (The Waterfront) ⓣ 0844 875 7575 ⓦ www.hiexpress.com

Hanover Hotel ££ This 18th-century bank-turned-hotel features live rock and blues bands most evenings in its McCartney's Bar, and is located in the heart of the city. ⓐ 62 Hanover St (Central Liverpool) ⓣ (0151) 709 6223 ⓦ www.hanover-hotel.co.uk

Hilton Liverpool ££ A new addition to the city's skyline, this modern hotel is at the heart of Liverpool's regenerating city centre and is within a short walk of all the attractions and sights along the riverside and central areas. ⊙ 3 Thomas Steers Way (The Waterfront) ☏ (0151) 708 4200 ⊛ www.hilton.co.uk

Malmaison ££ Exclusive and chic hotel chain featuring retro colours of browns and gothic purples in its décor, with furnishings that complement the funky rooms. Close to the Pier Head. ⊙ 7 William Jessop Way (The Waterfront) ☏ (0151) 229 5000 ⊛ www.malmaison-liverpool.com

Parr Street Hotel ££ A groovy, techno-rich, designer hotel that's housed above the famous Parr Street Studios, where herds of top stars have laid down tracks and can often be seen in the adjoining bar. Located in the heart of the bar and nightclub district. ⊙ 33–45 Parr St (Central Liverpool) ☏ (0151) 707 1050 ⊛ www.parrstreet.co.uk

Hard Days Night Hotel £££ Boutique hotel at the tip of the Cavern Quarter. All uber-modern rooms come with individual Beatles-related artwork, while the public areas are peppered with fascinating memorabilia. ⊙ North John St (Central Liverpool) ☏ (0151) 236 1964 ⊛ www.harddaysnighthotel.com

Hope Street Hotel £££ Multi-award-winning, luxury boutique hotel in the heart of the Georgian Quarter that oozes cool and sophistication and features one of the best restaurants in the northwest of England, The London Carriage Works (see page 100).

ⓐ 40 Hope St (The Georgian Quarter) ① (0151) 709 3000
ⓦ www.hopestreethotel.co.uk

APARTMENTS

Imagine Apartments ££ A selection of one- and two-bedroom apartments furnished in a modern style, located between the Georgian Quarter and the main shopping district.
ⓐ 69 Renshaw St (The Georgian Quarter) ① 07809 557302
ⓦ www.imagineapartments.com

Premier Apartments ££ Well-equipped self-catering apartments within a glass building in the newly built Eden Square Development. ⓐ 7 Hatton Garden (Central Liverpool)
① (0151) 227 9467 ⓦ www.premierapartmentsliverpool.com

HOSTELS

International Inn £ Converted Victorian warehouse in the heart of the action that combines hostel and apartment accommodation, Internet café, kitchen and TV lounge.
ⓐ 4 South Hunter St (The Georgian Quarter) ① (0151) 709 8135
ⓦ www.internationalinn.co.uk

YHA £ Purpose-built hostel close to the Albert Dock with all three-, four- and six-person rooms en-suite. A hearty buffet breakfast is included in the price. ⓐ 25 Tabley St (The Waterfront)
① 0845 371 9527 ⓦ www.yha.org.uk

THE BEST OF LIVERPOOL

Whatever your reason for coming and no matter how long you're staying, a colourful history, a prosperous present and an exciting future make Liverpool a fascinating place to visit.

TOP 10 ATTRACTIONS

- **The Three Graces** Nothing defines Liverpool more than these three iconic buildings on the Waterfront (see page 62).

- **Cavern Club** Not the original, but a faithful replica of the place where the fabulous foursome were at their wildest as a hot-and-sweaty live outfit. Its tiny stage still plays host to many a band (see page 74).

- **Ferry across the Mersey** Immortalised in song and film, this – one of the world's most famous river crossings – will put the city, its culture and its seafaring heritage into perspective (see page 58).

- **Merseyside Maritime Museum** Liverpool's long association with the sea is related via interactive displays and poignant exhibits (see page 62).

The Walker Art Gallery has one of the largest collections in England

- **International Slavery Museum** A comprehensive and thoughtful journey through both the city's dark past and the many social and economic issues confronting its inhabitants today (see page 65).

- **Walker Art Gallery** A fine collection of British and international art from the medieval period to the present day is shown in one of the city's grandest buildings (see page 80).

- **Tate Liverpool** Home to permanent and visiting exhibitions of some of the world's best contemporary and modern art (see page 66).

- **Liverpool Cathedral** The 'Great Space' is the country's largest cathedral and offers marvellous architecture and wonderful views from its tower (see page 95).

- **Liverpool Metropolitan Cathedral** Modernist building known locally as 'Paddy's Wigwam' that's famous for its coloured glass and a museum lying deep within the crypt (see page 96).

- **Anfield Football Stadium Tour** The home of Liverpool Football Club offers behind-the-scenes tours, access to the museum and a chance to sit on the touchline. For the faithful, this is a quasi-religious experience (see page 32).

Suggested itineraries

HALF-DAY: LIVERPOOL IN A HURRY

If time is of the essence, head for the Pier Head to marvel at the grand architecture of the Three Graces (see page 62) and catch one of the hourly **River Explorer ferries** (☎ (0151) 330 1444 ⓦ www.merseyferries.co.uk) that ply the Mersey. After this, take the short walk to the Albert Dock complex (see page 58) and admire the Tate, both inside and out (see page 66).

1 DAY: TIME TO SEE A LITTLE MORE

A full day means time to explore the museums located inside the Albert Dock. From there take one of the many guided tours on offer (see page 53), then stop off at the Cavern and Met Quarters (see pages 78 & 82) for a whole host of street entertainment, music memorabilia and shopping opportunities.

2–3 DAYS: TIME TO SEE MUCH MORE

Every aspect and area of the city can comfortably be seen – including Anfield (see page 32), the Walker Gallery (see page 80) and World Museum (see page 80) – with time in between to recover from the nightlife and rest those weary legs while chatting with locals in one of the legendary pubs. Those with a head for heights can visit the top of the Anglican Cathedral (see page 95) for a marvellous view of the city's ever-changing skyline while looking straight down on to the Georgian Quarter's intriguing mix of splendid architecture and well-known bars and eateries (see page 90).

LONGER: ENJOYING LIVERPOOL TO THE FULL

With so much time at your disposal, there are plenty of out-of-town destinations to enjoy. The Wirral (see page 106) offers marvellous and diverse attractions, fast-action water- and wind-sport venues and vast swathes of sandy beaches and parkland. By contrast, the Ribble Valley (see page 116) offers the tranquillity of verdant countryside and picturesque villages that seem to have changed little over the centuries.

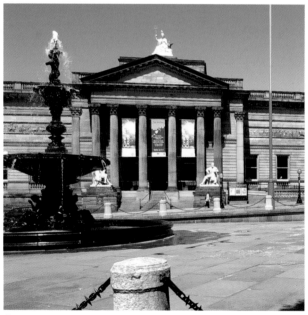

⬥ The Walker Gallery contains art treasures

Something for nothing

As John Winston Ono Lennon sang, the best things in life are free, and Liverpool offers plenty of attractions that don't necessitate parting with any money. By UK standards, the city is not particularly expensive and entrance to many of its museums and galleries is free of charge. On Mathew Street you'll find a number of street installations, including the **Liverpool Wall of Fame**, which features a disc for every number-one hit by local musicians. Close by are bricks etched with the names of bands who performed in the Cavern Club (see page 74) and an award-winning music-themed seat.

A pleasant, intimate and free source of spiritual solitude amid the hurly-burly of the city is **Our Lady and St Nicholas Church and Gardens**, near the Pier Head (ⓦ www.livpc.co.uk). Built on the one-time site of slave auctions, the church is regarded as the guardian of sailors departing from the port. The **Palm House** in

---

THE LIVE'SMART PASS

If you're planning to cram in as much as possible in a short time, it's worth buying the live'smart pass. This gives free admission to selected attractions, including The Beatles Story (see page 65), Liverpool FC Museum (see page 32) and the City Explorer Tour (see page 53). Valid for three days and costing around £30, the pass gets you free travel on the Mersey Ferry (see page 58) and city-centre bus loop as well as generous discounts in named restaurants. Visit ⓦ www.yourticketforliverpool.com for details.

● *Darwin monument at the Palm House in Sefton Park*

Sefton Park (Ⓦ www.palmhouse.org.uk) brings tropical flora to the city, while the surrounding greenery is a magnet for nature lovers, dog walkers and those simply out to enjoy the tranquillity of the mature trees and gardens. For those who like to walk and inhale bracing sea air, the promenade from the Pier Head (see page 62) offers fascinating views over the river to the Wirral; on the other side there is a riverside walk from Birkenhead to the small resort of New Brighton (see page 110 and visit Ⓦ www.merseytravel.gov.uk).

When it rains

Rain is a regular part of life in northwest England, particularly during the autumn and winter months when the wind and precipitation roll in off the Atlantic. However, as well as the various museums, galleries and shopping experiences in Liverpool, there are a number of other fascinating attractions to keep you sheltered from the elements.

Plumping for the **Cains Brewery Tour** (ⓐ Stanhope St ⓣ (0151) 709 8734 ⓦ www.cains.co.uk) can be justified on cultural grounds as its product is said to be the favourite beer of Quentin Tarantino. Located in an imposing Victorian building and using water sourced from the 'pool' in Liverpool, the company has been producing ale for over 150 years. This visit offers the chance to see not only the production process but also your interest rewarded with two free pints and a buffet.

Another fabulous rainy-day idea is a trip to the **National Conservation Centre** (ⓐ Whitechapel ⓣ (0151) 478 4999 ⓦ www.liverpoolmuseums.org.uk). Housed in a former railway warehouse, the centre provides an insight into how everything we see in museums and galleries is cared for by the conservationists and how skilfully they arrange and interpret objects to tell their stories. It also features superb photography-based exhibitions.

The **Western Approaches Museum** (ⓐ 1–3 Rumford St ⓣ (0151) 227 2008 ⓦ www.liverpoolwarmuseum.co.uk) offers an enthralling look at military life in wartime Liverpool. This top-secret underground headquarters was at the heart of operations during the Battle of the Atlantic in World War II.

Now reconstructed and refurnished according to its original specifications, you don't need to be interested in military history to enjoy this museum. A guided tour through the Williamson Tunnels (see page 103) is a unique experience. There are a number of opinions as to why the 19th-century merchant Williamson undertook this ambitious (and some would say bizarre) project, but as yet none has been conclusively confirmed.

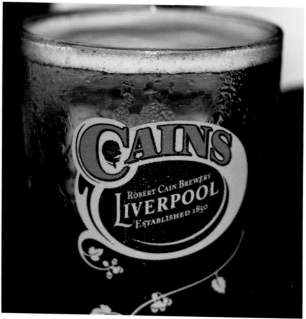

⏶ *Cains Brewery: top off the tour with a tasty tipple*

On arrival

TIME DIFFERENCE
Liverpool sets its clocks to Greenwich Mean Time (GMT) and puts them one hour forward from the end of March until the end of October for Daylight Saving Time.

ARRIVING
By air
Liverpool's **John Lennon Airport** (ⓐ Speke Hall Ave ⓣ 0871 521 8484 ⓦ www.liverpoolairport.com) is 14.5 km (9 miles) southeast of the city centre. Connecting the two is the **Airlink 500** bus service (ⓣ 0871 200 2233 ⓦ www.traveline.org.uk), which takes 45 minutes and operates from directly outside the South Terminal building.

⬢ *Liverpool Lime Street railway station*

Services begin at 06.45 and run every 30 minutes from Monday to Friday and every 30 minutes on evenings and weekends. An adult single fare costs about £2.50. The same journey in one of the many taxis that wait outside the terminal building takes about half the time and costs around £15.

By rail

Liverpool's primary mainline and local network railway station is the central **Liverpool Lime Street** (☏ 0845 748 4950). Regular daily services run to all the major British cities operated by Northern Rail, Virgin Trains, TransPennine Express and Central Trains. For tickets, timetables and real-time running times, visit **National Rail Enquiries** at ⊛ www.nationalrail.co.uk

By road

Getting to the city by coach is a great budget option, with express services from most British towns and cities, including a half-hourly service from Manchester and a coach every two hours to and from London. All coaches arriving in Liverpool use the centrally located **National Express Coach Station** (@ Norton St ☏ 0871 781 8181 ⊛ www.nationalexpress.com).

There are four main motorway routes leading into Liverpool: the M53 and M56 (via Manchester Airport) enter from the south, with access to Chester and North Wales; the M62 runs from Hull on the east coast and arrives in the middle of the city; the M58 enters the city from the north. All are connected to the motorway network via the M6.

Pay parking is plentiful early in the day but is soon snapped up, particularly on Saturdays. The city council operates a number of 'pay

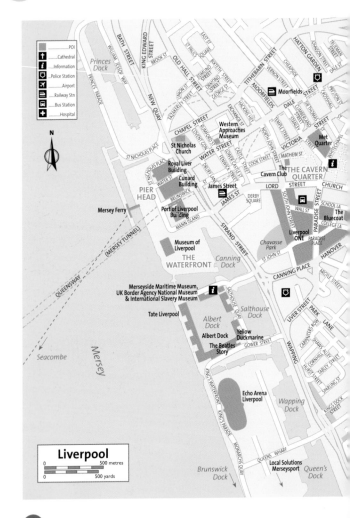

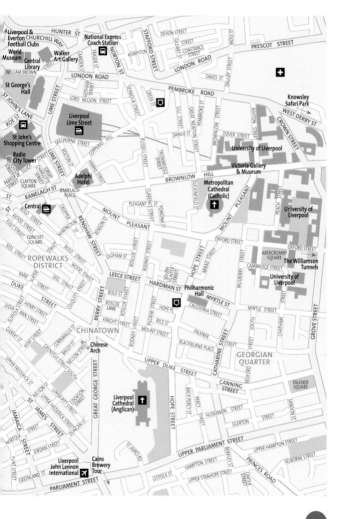

and display' on- and off-street parking areas. Parking restrictions are strictly enforced and traffic wardens take no prisoners.

By water

There are daily ferry services between Dublin and Liverpool (Birkenhead, on the Wirral), with a journey time of around seven hours. Services between Belfast and Liverpool (Birkenhead) take an hour longer. Booking tickets online and in advance is generally cheaper, and this can be done through **Norfolkline** (ⓐ 12 Quays Terminal, Tower Rd, Birkenhead, Wirral ❶ 0844 499 0007 ⓦ www.norfolkline.com). A ferry service also operates between the Isle of Man and the Pier Head in the city centre. The service is run by the **Isle of Man Steam Packet Company** (ⓐ Princes Parade ❶ 0871 222 1333 ⓦ www.steam-packet.com).

FINDING YOUR FEET

As in any major city, visitors should be mindful of pickpockets in crowded areas. While much of the centre has been pedestrianised (particularly the main shopping district), there are still busy roads that have to be negotiated and it's safest to use pedestrian crossings. If you get lost, almost all locals will be happy to give directions.

ORIENTATION

A number of landmarks make the city easy to navigate, not least the River Mersey, which marks its western boundary. The Metropolitan Cathedral (see page 96) marks the eastern boundary; to the south, the city centre extends to Liverpool Cathedral (see page 95), while to the north the Walker Gallery (see page 80) and World Museum (see page 80) are good boundary markers. A useful

TAKING A TOUR

An enjoyable way of seeing Liverpool's major sights is to take an organised bus tour. **Beatles Magical Mystery Tour** (ⓣ (0151) 236 9091 ⓦ www.cavernclub.org) runs a two-hour coach excursion around Beatles-related sights. **City Explorer** (ⓣ (0151) 922 4284 ⓦ www.cityexplorerliverpool.co.uk) offers 50-minute sightseeing tours with commentary throughout the summer, while **City Sightseeing** (ⓣ (0151) 203 3920 ⓦ www.city-sightseeing.com) provides hop-on and -off open-top double-decker bus tours every half-hour throughout the year.

meeting point is the Radio City Tower (formerly St John's Tower) in Houghton Street in the heart of the city. A concrete beacon standing high above the city, it can be seen for miles.

GETTING AROUND

Despite the plethora of transport options, walking is the best way to see the city. You could expect to cross its centre east to west on foot in 20 to 25 minutes, with a similar timing north to south.

Fast, frequent and reliable trains operate across the whole of Merseyside and beyond, as do local bus services, which continually circle the city. These are free to anyone holding a valid train ticket or live'smart pass (see page 44). For more information regarding all routes, timetables and fares, consult **Merseytravel** (ⓣ 0871 200 2233 ⓦ www.merseytravel.gov.uk).

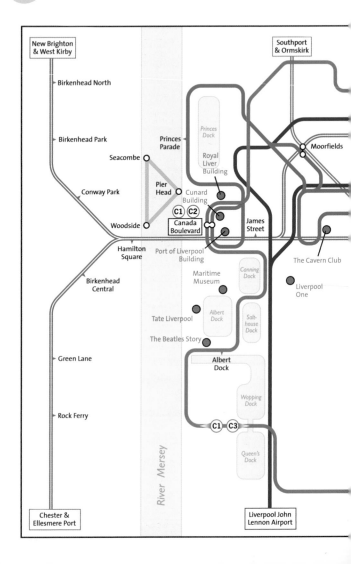

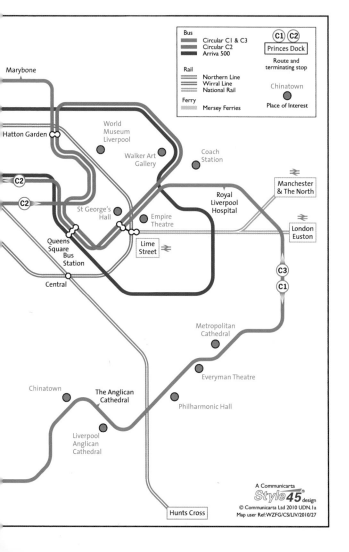

Black (hackney) cabs are plentiful and can be either hailed on the street or picked up from the designated taxi ranks at Lime Street Station (see page 49), **James Street Station** (ⓐ James St), the Britannia Adelphi Hotel (see page 37), Whitechapel, Sir Thomas Street and Chinatown. Increased demand after 23.00 at weekends makes booking advisable – this can be done via ① (0151) 298 2222 ⓦ www.merseycabs.co.uk. There are also a number of private hire companies in the city that operate on a pre-booking system only. The main ones are:

Davy Liver Taxis ① (0151) 708 7080 ⓦ www.davylivertaxis.co.uk
Excel Radio Cars ① (0151) 728 8888
Liverpool Taxis ① (0151) 223 0039 ⓦ www.taxiliverpool.co.uk

CAR HIRE

For exploring the city, car hire is only really necessary for those with mobility challenges. However, for visiting regions beyond the city limits, hiring a car can, for some, be a preferable alternative to public transport. Some reliable companies are:

Arnold Clark ⓐ 131 Sefton St, Toxteth ① (0151) 708 5330
ⓦ www.arnoldclarkrental.com
Enterprise ⓐ Arrivals Hall, Liverpool John Lennon Airport
① (0151) 486 6600 ⓦ www.enterprise.co.uk
Europcar ⓐ 278 East Prescott Rd, Knotty Ash ① (0151) 551 8205
ⓦ www.europcar.co.uk
Hertz ⓐ 141 Vauxhall Rd ① (0151) 227 2222 ⓦ www.hertz.com

● *The ferry making its way across the Mersey to Birkenhead*

THE CITY OF
Liverpool

The Waterfront

The Waterfront extends all along the River Mersey, but it's the stretch bordering the city centre that draws most visitors. Separated from the centre by the busy street known as the Strand, the remarkable development of this World Heritage Site shows no sign of abating. The Waterfront is a nesting place for the local rich and famous, and its fashionable bars, clubs and restaurants reflect the renewed aspirations of the city and its people. The area is eminently walkable, but if you decide to take public transport, buses S1, S2 and S3 cover it comprehensively.

SIGHTS & ATTRACTIONS

Albert Dock

Many of the Waterfront attractions (including the ones in this chapter) are located within the huge, brick-built Albert Dock edifice, a building that has been at the forefront of Liverpool's latest renaissance. Ⓦ www.albertdock.com Ⓝ Bus: 11, S1; Train: Moorfields Station is a five-minute walk away

Mersey Ferry

One of the most famous river journeys in the world, taking the ferry across the Mersey is a must-do experience, if only to get a view of the famous waterfront and gain a perspective on just why the river has been so important to Liverpool for the past 800 years. The full round-trip cruise lasts for 50 minutes and is accompanied by a commentary. Ⓐ Departs from the Pier Head

⬧ *A clipper moored in Albert Dock*

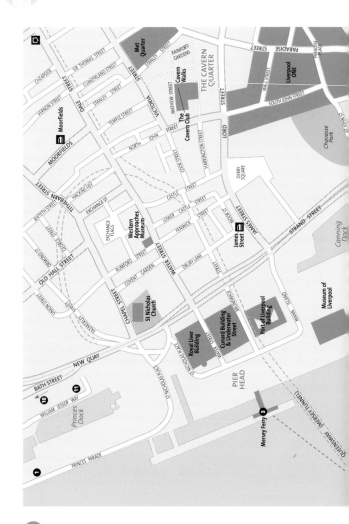

Met Quarter

Cavern Walks

THE CAVERN QUARTER

The Cavern Club

Liverpool ONE

Chavasse Park

Moorfields

Western Approaches Museum

St Nicholas Church

James Street

Strand Street

Canning Dock

Royal Liver Building

Cunard Building & Underwater Street

Port of Liverpool Building

Museum of Liverpool

PIER HEAD

New Quay

Bath Street

Princes Dock

Mersey Ferry

QUEENSWAY (MERSEY TUNNEL)

Princes Parade

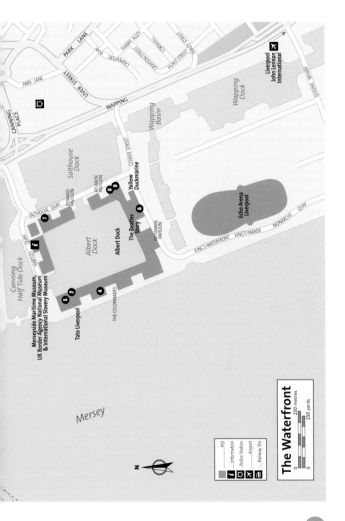

PARK LANE

PARK LANE

LIVER STREET

CARPENTERS ROW

GRAYSON STREET

CORNHILL

HURST STREET

TABLEY STREET

Liverpool
John Lennon
International

QUEENS WHARF

CANNING PLACE

WAPPING

WAPPING

Wapping
Dock

Wapping
Basin

Salthouse
Dock

COVER STREET

EDWARD
PAVILION

ATLANTIC
PAVILION

8

8

Yellow
Duckmarine

6

SALTHOUSE QUAY

7

HARTLEY QUAY

Albert
Dock

Albert Dock

The Beatles
Story

BRITANNIA
PAVILION

KING'S WATERFRONT

KING'S PARADE

MONARCHS QUAY

Echo Arena
Liverpool

Canning
Half Tide Dock

Merseyside Maritime Museum,
UK Border Agency National Museum
& International Slavery Museum

Tate Liverpool

5

2

4

THE COLONNADES

Mersey

N

The Waterfront

		POI
		Information
		Police Station
		Airport
		Railway Stn

0   250 metres
0   250 yards

📞 (0151) 330 1444 🌐 www.merseyferries.co.uk 🕐 Cruises on the hour 10.00–15.00 Mon–Fri, 10.00–18.00 Sat & Sun ⓘ Admission charge

Merseyside Maritime Museum

Housed in a former warehouse by the Albert Dock, the museum takes visitors on an exploration through Liverpool's famous seafaring heritage. Spread over four floors, the audio and visual collections cover everything from the city's humble maritime aspirations through to its pivotal role during World War II. Highlights include the tragic stories of three ships, the *Titanic*, *Lusitania* and *Empress*, all of which had strong connections to the city. 🅐 Hartley Quay, Albert Dock 📞 (0151) 478 4499 🌐 www.liverpoolmuseums.org.uk 🕐 10.00–17.00 daily

Pier Head

Of immense symbolic meaning to the city, the Pier Head is not only the embarkation point for the Mersey Ferry, but also the home of the **Three Graces** – the Cunard Building, Liver Building and Port of Liverpool Building. These grand icons were designed loosely to mirror the appearance of Chicago's waterfront skyline and have defined the city visually for a century. As private offices they are not open to the public.

UK Border Agency National Museum or 'Seized!'

Although the tone is at times a little preachy, this museum is an interesting, hands-on place to spend an hour discovering the story of smuggling and the lengths people will go to make money illegally. 🅐 Hartley Quay, Albert Dock 📞 (0151) 478 4499 🌐 www.liverpoolmuseums.org.uk 🕐 10.00–17.00 daily

THE LIVER BIRDS

Two of Liverpool's most emblematic figures are perched
90 m (295 ft) above the ground on top of the Liver Building
at the Pier Head. The building stretches up a lofty 13 floors,
and, on its completion in 1911, was regarded as Britain's
first skyscraper.

There is still much debate as to the true origin of the
unique species of these two birds. The original emblem of
the city was an eagle found on the seal of King John, who,
in 1207, granted Liverpool its first charter. Unfortunately,
during a Civil War siege in 1644, the seal was mislaid and
subsequent designs reflected ignorance or artistic
shortcomings: most resembled a mutant cormorant.

The design for the birds on show today resulted from
an international competition won by Carl Bernard Bartels,
a German sculptor. Made of copper, both stand 5.5 m (18 ft)
tall, with wingspans of 7.3 m (24 ft). Each raffishly carries
a sprig of foliage in its beak. Legend has it that if the birds
were to take flight, the city would perish. Any anxiety
caused by that is assuaged by another superstition that
the birds will only flap their wings if a virgin or an honest
Liverpudlian should pass the building. The female looks
wistfully out to sea for returning sailors; on the opposite
side of the building the male looks inland and is said to
be keeping a hopeful eye out for the opening of the
pub doors.

The Port of Liverpool Building at the Pier Head

Yellow Duckmarine

This former World War II landing craft takes you on a guided and informative tour of the city streets as well as plunging into the waters of the Salthouse and Albert Dock. Good fun if not notably subtle. ⓐ The Anchor Courtyard, Albert Dock ⓣ (0151) 708 7799 ⓦ www.theyellowduckmarine.co.uk ⓛ 10.30–dusk daily ⓘ Admission charge

CULTURE

The Beatles Story

Aficionados should dedicate at least two hours to this celebration of the band. Even those with only a passing interest will still find plenty to capture their imagination, particularly if they opt for the Living History audio guide. ⓐ Britannia Pavilion, Albert Dock ⓣ (0151) 709 1963 ⓦ www.beatlesstory.com ⓛ 09.00–19.00 daily ⓘ Admission charge

International Slavery Museum

This successful combination of the inspirational and the tragic is dominated by the issues of slavery, human rights, cultural identity and racism. The museum doesn't shy away from the less glorious events in Liverpool's history. ⓐ Hartley Quay, Albert Dock ⓣ (0151) 478 4499 ⓦ www.liverpoolmuseums.org.uk ⓛ 10.00–17.00 daily

Museum of Liverpool

Located on the iconic waterfront, this new museum tells the tale of this unique city, its people and the impact Merseyside has had on the world, all told through an innovative array of engaging multimedia. This is also the new home of the Open Eye Gallery, which showcases photographic and audiovisual work. ⓐ Pier Head ⓣ (0151) 207 0001 ⓦ www.liverpoolmuseums.org.uk ⓛ Still to be confirmed

Tate Liverpool

Housed in a beautifully converted warehouse, this is one of the biggest galleries for modern and contemporary art outside London. Home to northern England's national collection of modern art and a regular venue for prestigious peripatetic exhibitions, luminaries such as Lichtenstein, Dalí, Hockney and Gilbert and George have all had exhibitions here. ⓐ The Colonnades, Albert Dock ⓣ (0151) 702 7400 ⓦ www.tate.org.uk ⓛ 10.00–17.50 daily (June–Aug); 10.00–17.50 Tues–Sun (Sept–May)

RETAIL THERAPY

Shopping opportunities along the Waterfront are concentrated within the Albert Dock complex (see page 58), which is sheltered from the elements within covered, ground-floor colonnades. The overriding retail theme here is art, as found in **The Freshwater Gallery** (ⓐ 15 The Colonnades, Albert Dock ⓣ (0151) 707 7991), **BEE Artistic** (ⓐ The Colonnades, Albert Dock ⓣ (0151) 707 6990) and the Tate shop (see above). For prints connected to all things Liverpool (especially maritime), **Liverpool Pictures and Print** (ⓐ 5 The Colonnades, Albert Dock ⓣ (0151) 709 3566 ⓦ www.liverpoolpictures.co.uk) has the solution. The shop at the Maritime Museum (see page 62) sells everything from pencils to glossy hardback books. Those in search of something a little more kitsch should visit **Nature's Treasures** (ⓐ Albert Dock ❶ (0151) 709 4492) for crystals and minerals and **Wizzard** (ⓐ Albert Dock ❶ (0151) 709 0113) for novelties. For that sugar rush and energy boost between meals, **Quay Confectionery** (ⓐ Albert Dock ❶ (0151) 709 0530) supplies all forms of sticky sweets and drinks. For picnic ingredients, **Vinea** (ⓐ Albert Dock ❶ (0151) 707 8962) provides food and wine from around the world courtesy of its shop and deli. The massive Liverpool ONE shopping centre, just across the road from the Waterfront, houses many high-street stores, with fashion clothing particularly well represented. Its website – www.liverpool-one.com – has listings and details of them all. Also here is the **LFC Store** (ⓐ 7 South John St ❶ (0151) 709 4345), a paradise for Reds fans in search of club-related fashion, gifts, souvenirs and accessories in the world's largest football megastore.

TAKING A BREAK

Coffee Union £ ❶ A local institution that takes its java very seriously by importing carefully chosen beans direct from ethical producers. This small branch is one of five throughout the city and also offers soup and a variety of sandwiches. ⓐ 12 Princes Parade, Princes Dock ❶ (0151) 227 1600 ❶ 07.00–15.00 Mon–Fri

La Crepe Rit £ ❷ Overlooking the Albert Dock, this French-style café serves savoury and sweet pancakes, together with an assortment of coffees and drinks. ⓐ 20 The Colonnades ❶ (0151) 709 9444 ❶ 10.30–17.00 daily

Mersey Ferry £ ❸ Although the on-board offerings are unlikely to win a Michelin star, a seat on the deck while you take in the views and commentary with a reviving hot drink is a pleasant way to take a breather (see page 58). ⓐ Pier Head

Nosh £ ❹ A popular and smart café with external quayside seating offering simple and affordable full English breakfasts along with light lunches of filled jacket potatoes, soup and sandwiches. ⓐ 11 The Colonnades, Albert Dock ⓣ (0151) 709 0909 ⓛ 09.30–17.30 daily

Tate Café £ ❺ An ideal pit stop between injections of culture in the gallery next door. This is a large, bright and colourful venue offering tasty contemporary menus (including afternoon tea). ⓐ The Colonnades, Albert Dock ⓣ (0151) 702 7581 ⓛ 10.00–17.30 daily (June–Aug); 10.00–17.30 Tues–Sun (Sept–May)

AFTER DARK

RESTAURANTS

Circo £ ❻ Cavernous, quirky restaurant-bar that draws on European circus themes for its cabaret, décor and ambience and New York steakhouses for its menu. All this is complemented by a creative and extensive cocktail list. ⓐ Britannia Pavilion, Albert Dock ⓣ (0151) 709 0470 ⓦ www.circoliverpool.com ⓛ 10.00–01.00 Mon–Thur, 10.00–02.00 Fri & Sat, 10.00–00.30 Sun

Gusto ££ ❼ In the heart of Albert Dock, this stylish Italian restaurant offers the attraction of watching made-to-order pizzas being pounded and flung in the air. Pasta, grills and seafood are also on the menu, as is a fine selection of Italian wines and cocktails. ⓐ Edward Pavilion, Albert Dock ⓣ (0151) 708 6969 ⓦ www.gustorestaurants.uk.com ⓛ 12.00–23.00 daily

▲ Take a break at the Tate Café

Ha! Ha! Bar & Canteen ££ ❶ The emphasis here is on seasonal produce sourced whenever possible from the UK to create simple, well-presented fare. There are splendid waterside views from the terrace space; the interior comes dressed in minimalist industrial chic with splashes of autumnal shades. ⓐ Atlantic Pavilion, Albert Dock ❶ (0151) 707 7877 ⓦ www.hahaonline.co.uk ❶ 10.00–23.00 Mon–Sat, 10.00–22.00 Sun

⬥ *A taste of Anglo-French finesse at Malmaison Brasserie*

Spice Lounge ££ ❾ Opulent Indian restaurant that steers clear of dishes familiar to British palates and offers instead cuisine of the type actually found in India. Spices are imported every few weeks and then ground and roasted on-site while the décor adds to the authenticity with dark woods and rich crimsons. ⓐ Atlantic Pavilion, Albert Dock ⓣ (0151) 707 2202 ⓦ www.spicelounge.uk.com ⓛ 12.00–24.00 daily

Elude Bar and Restaurant £££ ❿ This intimate and sophisticated candlelit restaurant is housed within a former potato warehouse in a rundown docklands area. Regardless of the geography, the atmosphere is romantic, the furniture and adornments antique, and the food is stylishly presented modern and classic European. ⓐ 15 Porter St ⓣ (0151) 227 3882 ⓦ www.eludeliverpool.com ⓛ 18.30–21.30 Thur–Sat

Malmaison Brasserie £££ ⓫ Foodies will find this a treat. A chic, cosmopolitan hotel eatery that offers innovative and contemporary French and British food prepared with love and occasional humour. The 'Homegrown and Local' menu features the finest Lancashire and Cheshire produce. If the evening price is a bit rich, lunches are excellent value. ⓐ William Jessop Way, Princes Dock ⓣ (0151) 229 5000 ⓦ www.malmaison-liverpool.com ⓛ 18.30–22.00 daily

PUBS

The Baltic Fleet One of the few remaining traditional dockside pubs and a characterful change from the trendiness of Albert Dock. Although in need of a little superficial love and attention,

○ *The Albert Dock's famous Pumphouse Inn*

this maritime-themed venue is a paradise for real-ale drinkers. It has its own brewery in the cellar that shares space with tunnels that are said to be the remnants of smuggling activity. ⓐ Wapping High St ⓣ (0151) 709 3116 ⓞ 11.00–23.00 Sun–Tues, 11.00–24.00 Wed–Sat

The Pumphouse Inn Originally built in 1870, this gem of industrial heritage has been carefully restored to provide a relaxed ambience, both within its brick structure and

on the large terrace overlooking the Waterfront sights.
ⓐ Albert Dock ⓣ (0151) 709 2367 ⓛ 10.00–24.00 daily

BARS & CLUBS

Blue Bar and Comedy Central Music, comedy and a range of
live events make this fashionably popular comedy and music
venue, bar and restaurant with the city's glitterati. Housed over
three levels, this former 19th-century waterfront warehouse
also comes with a terrace to witness the maritime and celeb
comings and goings. ⓐ Edward Pavilion, Albert Dock ⓣ (0151) 702
5834 ⓦ www.bluebarliverpool.co.uk ⓛ Blue Bar: 11.00–03.00
daily; Comedy Central: 20.00–23.00 Thur–Sat

Pan American Club One of the city's most fashionable joints
and a magnet for stars of stage, screen and football pitch. This
contemporary late-night bar offers the options of zoning out
with a cocktail among its suave leather booths, parading on the
dance floor to funk, Latin and salsa or whooping it up courtesy
of one of the regular live acts. The menu concentrates on classic
regional American dining. ⓐ Albert Dock ⓣ (0151) 702 5831
ⓦ www.panambarliverpool.co.uk ⓛ 11.00–03.00 daily

Portico Cantina & Bar Service is friendly and with gusto while
the food served draws less from traditional Mexican and more
on Tex-Mex. Cocktails are extravagant with well-sourced and
quality ingredients and the décor draws on both the rustic and
maritime. ⓐ 8 Britannia Pavilion, Albert Dock ⓣ (0151) 706 7400
ⓦ www.porticocantina.co.uk ⓛ 11.00–22.00 Sun–Thur,
11.00–23.00 Fri & Sat

Central Liverpool

The heart of Liverpool is a mosaic of differing architectural styles, some handsome and interesting, some whose beauty probably lies in their usefulness. Where once the pulse of the city was powered by its docklands, these days Liverpudlians do most of their working, shopping and dancing in the central district.

The buildings and activities of the city centre have traditionally been – and to some extent still are – related to the world of finance. Fine, early 20th-century office buildings such as those found on Water, Castle and James Streets are still used for their original purpose; when they empty at the end of the working day or at the weekend, the area can take on the feel of a ghost town. Moving easterly and uphill away from the River Mersey, the rise on the landscape at the top of James Street marks the site of Liverpool's long-gone castle. Although there is little of note along the 1970s redevelopment of the main shopping streets of Lord and Church, and Williamson Square, the surrounding Ropewalks District and The Cavern Quarter have plenty going for them in terms of daytime interest and nightlife.

Although the S2 and S3 bus services will bring you close to city-centre attractions, by far the best and most enjoyable way of getting around this area is to walk.

SIGHTS & ATTRACTIONS

The Cavern Club

The original site of the legendary venue now lies buried beneath the boutique emporium of Cavern Walks. Eighteen stone cellar

🔺 *The Cavern Club – Liverpool's musical crucible*

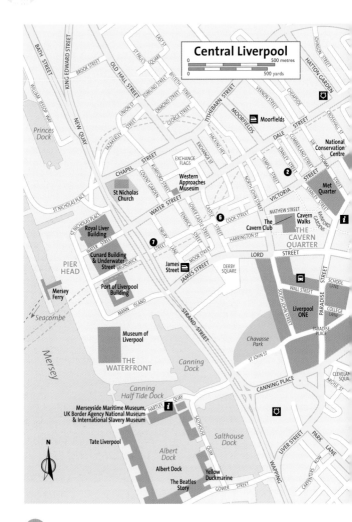

Central Liverpool

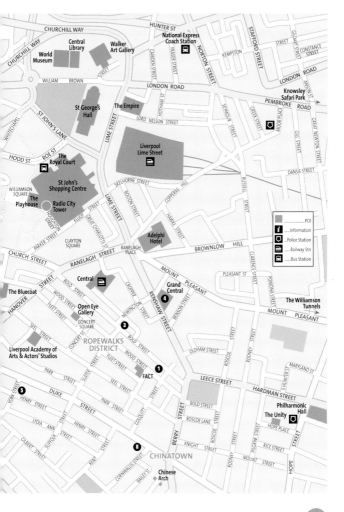

THE CAVERN QUARTER

With Mathew Street and Beatles associations at its heart, it's little wonder this area draws visitors to the city. In the warmer months, the streets can be packed at weekends with a multitude of camera-wielding tourists and fancy-dressed hen and stag parties. This area is also home to some of the city's most exclusive shopping. When evening falls, the decorative canopy of street lights flickers into life and the bars, clubs and pubs pump up the volume. Venues celebrating the music of recent and not-so-recent periods are heavy on the ground, so if your prime shape-throwing era falls anywhere between the 1960s and the present day, you'll be well catered for.

steps led down to it when it first opened its doors to a jazz crowd in 1957, but it was The Beatles who were to make the dark, low-ceilinged club famous. They performed there 274 times between 1961 and 1963. It finally closed its doors in 1973. A few metres along the street, this replica club has since been built. ⓐ 10 Mathew St ⓘ (0151) 236 1965 ⓦ www.cavernclub.org ⓛ 11.00–20.00 Mon–Wed, 11.00–02.00 Thur, 11.00–02.30 Fri & Sat, 11.00–00.30 Sun ❶ Admission charge Sat & Sun after 18.00

St George's Hall

The first building to greet passengers emerging from the front entrance of Lime Street Station is arguably the finest neoclassical building in Europe. It first opened in 1854 after a long campaign by the city's population for a place in which to hold regular music events. The architect, Harvey Lonsdale Elmes, had the intriguing idea of combining a concert hall and a set of assize courts under the same roof. In 2007, a massive restoration project was completed, and if you take a tour you'll see reconstructed holding cells, the criminal court and the great hall. The large spaces to the front of the building are looked over by statues of prominent Victorians, and on special occasions there are outdoor concerts. ⓐ William Brown St ⓣ (0151) 225 6909 ⓦ www.stgeorgesliverpool.co.uk ⓛ 10.00–17.00 Tues–Sat

CULTURE

The Bluecoat

One of the oldest and most visually stunning buildings in the city, this former school is now a centre for contemporary performances and visual art and a meeting place for local artists. The 'secret' garden at the rear and the courtyard to the front are popular places to take a breather. ⓐ School Lane ⓣ (0151) 702 5324 ⓦ www.thebluecoat.org.uk ⓛ 10.00–18.00 daily

FACT

This combination of cinema and new media galleries has an ever-changing programme of challenging and quirky installations together with screenings of the latest releases from the major studios and smaller independents. ⓐ 88 Wood St ⓣ (0151) 707 4464 ⓦ www.fact.co.uk ⓛ Centre: 10.00–23.00 Mon–Fri, 11.00–22.30 Sat & Sun; galleries & media lounge: 11.00–18.00 Mon–Fri, 12.00–18.00 Sat & Sun

The Liverpool Academy of Arts

Tucked away on the city centre's periphery, the unlikely looking
building (it's a former large retail space) is home to a renowned
tradition of continually changing art and sculpture work created
by locals. Next door is an 80-seat fringe theatre (see page 89).
ⓐ 32 Seel St ⓣ (0151) 709 0735 ⓦ www.la-art.co.uk
ⓛ 11.00–17.00 daily

Walker Art Gallery

This grand 19th-century building is home to internationally
important collections of art dating from the 14th century to
the present day. Its exhibits include masterpieces by Rembrandt,
Degas, Poussin, Gainsborough and Hopper. ⓐ William Brown St
ⓣ (0151) 478 4199 ⓦ www.liverpoolmuseums.org.uk
ⓛ 10.00–17.00 daily

World Museum

The pterodactyl hanging in the atrium only hints at the
delights within. The eclectic collection of scientific, natural-
world and cultural items offers something for everyone and
is particularly engrossing if you like to get hands-on and
interactive with exhibits. ⓐ William Brown St ⓣ (0151) 478 4393
ⓦ www.liverpoolmuseums.org.uk ⓛ 10.00–17.00 daily

RETAIL THERAPY

The Beatles Shop All the Fab Four memorabilia and merchandise
you could shake Ringo's drumstick at. Open for nearly 30 years,
this lively and enduring basement cave boasts 'the largest range

◔ The Bluecoat offers art and performance in a classical setting

of Beatles gear in the world' and is located at the epicentre of Beatledom, Mathew Street. ⓐ 31 Mathew Street ⓣ (0151) 236 8066 ⓦ www.thebeatleshop.co.uk ⓛ 09.30–17.30 Mon–Sat, 10.30–16.30 Sun

Cricket Justine Mills, the owner of this famous independent designer boutique for men and women, has been supplying the fashion-conscious with her bold collections for nearly 20 years. It's not unusual to see paparazzi snaps of stars carrying her trademark zebra- and leopard-print bags. ⓐ Cavern Walks ⓣ (0151) 227 4645 ⓦ www.cricketliverpool.co.uk ⓛ 09.30–17.30 Mon–Sat, 12.00–16.00 Sun

Grand Central A former religious meeting hall and (secular) cinema, this is now a great destination for those interested in purchasing items alternative, designer, retro and even paranormal. ⓐ 35 Renshaw St ⓛ 10.00–17.30 Mon–Sat

Met Quarter A style-savvy indoor mall that's home to internationally branded clothing, jewellery and accessory stores and is only a handbag's throw from the similarly themed stores of Cavern Walks. There is a small selection of cafés where you can rest your weary credit card. ⓐ Whitechapel ⓣ (0151) 224 2390 ⓦ www.metquarter.me.uk ⓛ 09.30–18.00 Mon–Sat, 11.00–17.00 Sun

Probe Records A legendarily big (and independent) player in Liverpool's musical and underground scene for decades. The friendly and well-informed staff lead vinyl junkies

through oceans of records, both new and reissued.
🅐 The Bluecoat, School Lane 🅣 (0151) 708 8815
🅦 www.probe-records.com 🕐 10.00–18.00 Mon–Sat

TAKING A BREAK

Café Tabac £ ❶ A great place to enjoy reasonably priced coffee, sandwiches and salads. The Boho furnishings and cool colour tones create a relaxed ambience, and the large window makes it an ideal spot for people-watching. 🅐 126 Bold St
🅣 (0151) 709 9502 🅦 www.cafetabac.co.uk 🕐 09.00–23.00 Mon–Fri, 09.00–24.00 Sat, 10.00–23.00 Sun

Delifonseca £ ❷ Whether you seek coffee and cake, a takeaway sandwich, a selection of fine international cheeses and meats or a full three-course lunch, this place has it all. 🅐 12 Stanley St
🅣 (0151) 255 0808 🅦 www.delifonseca.co.uk 🕐 08.00–21.00 Mon–Sat

The Egg Café £ ❸ Popular with vegetarians, vegans, students and alternative types (and also with non-alternative carnivores), this is a pleasant, unpretentious place serving vegetarian food. 🅐 2nd floor, 16–18 Newington St 🅣 (0151) 707 2755 🕐 09.00–22.30 daily

Mandy Moo's £ ❹ A pop-culture-themed café specialising in excellent milkshakes and ice creams and overlooking the tranquil Roscoe Gardens. 🅐 Grand Central, 35 Renshaw St
🕐 10.00–17.30 Mon–Sat

THE ADELPHI HOTEL

The current structure of this cult venue (now officially called the Britannia Adelphi Hotel) was built in 1914 by Arthur Towle, who spared no expense in making it one of the most luxurious and eye-catching hotels in Europe. Solid marble, wood panelling and coloured glass were liberally used in its grand public rooms and bedrooms, while its Sefton Suite mirrored the first-class smoking lounge of the SS *Titanic*. Was that an omen? Among the many famous guests who stopped by to join the great ocean liners en route to America in the hotel's salad days were Roy Rogers and his horse, Trigger, who was left to trot the corridors on his own.

AFTER DARK

RESTAURANTS

Christakis £ ❾ This is an affordable, lively and enduringly popular Greek restaurant on three floors, featuring boisterous entertainment such as dancing, belly dancers and – rarer these days – plate smashing. The traditional food is lovingly prepared by Greek Cypriot chefs and the menu includes a selection of Olympian-proportioned banquets. Children are very welcome and a number of early-bird specials and loyalty incentives make for a cheap and lively night out. ❸ 7 York St
❶ (0151) 708 7377 ⓦ www.christakisgreektaverna.com
🕐 14.00–24.00 Mon–Fri, 16.00–02.00 Sat & Sun

As the liner traffic diminished, however, so did the hotel's fortunes. In 1997, its tribulations became part of the public consciousness when the BBC filmed a 'fly-on-the-wall' series called *Hotel*. Eleven million viewers tuned in weekly and bookings increased by 20 per cent, despite the sometimes psychotic behaviour on display. Some of the staff became household names and a glut of spin-off memorabilia was unleashed, including a single, *Just cook, will yer?* This new kind of fame may well have been Faustian: the Adelphi is now a rather tired and eccentric creature who, while her glory days may be over, at least maintains her original form. The Adelphi's still big; maybe it's the hotel, catering and leisure industry that got small.

The Olive Press £ ❻ Friendly and informal, The Olive Press has become a byword for quality Italian favourites. Stone-baked pizzas, pasta – or, for the more flushed of wallet, lobster – are the specialities. ⓐ 25–27 Castle St ⓣ (0151) 227 2242 ⓦ www.heathcotes.co.uk ⓛ 11.45–22.00 Mon–Sat, 11.45–21.00 Sun

Meet ££ ❼ The first Argentinian restaurant in town, this really is one for ravenous carnivores. Huge cuts of quality meat are skilfully and simply prepared in the open kitchen and, while the menu is not extensive, there are some fish and seafood options. Despite the fleshly theme, vegetarians do get a nod of acknowledgement. ⓐ 50 Brunswick St ⓣ (0151) 258 1816

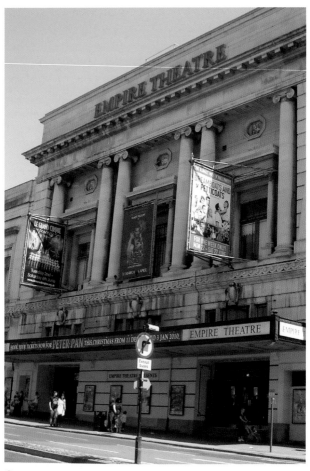

⬥ The Empire is the largest theatre in Liverpool

ⓦ www.meetrestaurant.co.uk ⓛ 12.00–23.00 Mon–Fri, 17.00–23.00 Sat & Sun

Savina ££ ⓞ Traditional and contemporary Mexican food served in modern, minimalistic surroundings. The menu choices stretch beyond the usual gringo fare found elsewhere and the jalapeños really pack an eye-watering punch. ⓐ 138 Duke St ⓣ (0151) 708 9095 ⓦ www.savinarestaurant.co.uk ⓛ 17.00–23.00 Mon–Fri, 13.00–23.00 Sat & Sun

PUBS

The Grapes Unpretentious watering hole among the themed bars and clubs of The Cavern Quarter that attracts locals and Beatles fans: this is where the boys came to relax with a pint after playing at the Cavern Club. ⓐ 25 Mathew St ⓣ (0151) 255 1525 ⓛ 12.00–01.00 daily

The Vines Known locally as 'The Big House', this is a wonderfully classic Edwardian-era pub with exuberant Baroque architecture and beer from the local Cains Brewery (see page 46). ⓐ 81 Lime St ⓣ (0151) 709 3977 ⓛ 12.00–24.00 Mon–Thur, 09.00–02.00 Fri & Sat, 09.00–24.00 Sun

The White Star This is another pub that the Beatles frequented, though it also pays tribute to the White Star Shipping Line and comes with some handsome Victorian furnishings and Lancashire real ale. Four chairs in the back room bear the Beatles' nameplates. ⓐ 2 Rainford Gardens ⓣ (0151) 231 6861 ⓛ 11.00–23.00 daily

BARS & CLUBS

Alma de Cuba Housed in a former church, this dramatic, candlelit, national-award-winning venue retains many of the original ecclesiastical features. Innovative cuisine tips a nod to the Caribbean, or you can simply have a drink, gasp at the interior and enjoy the live music. ⓐ 90 Seel St ⓣ (0151) 702 7394 ⓦ www.alma-de-cuba.com ⓛ 11.00–02.00 daily

Korova A hub and hangout for musical legends past and present who come to catch the latest live acts, mix with civilians or take to the decks. There are three distinct areas – boothed bar, basement club with stage, and café serving Latino-style food. ⓐ 32 Hope St ⓣ (0151) 709 7097 ⓦ www.korova-liverpool.com ⓛ 11.00–02.00 Mon–Sat, 11.00–00.30 Sun

The Krazy House Spread over three themed floors in one of the largest venues of its kind, this aptly named club mixes specialist DJs and live bands to create fantastically enjoyable mayhem. ⓐ 16 Wood St ⓣ (0151) 708 5016 ⓦ www.thekrazyhouse.co.uk ⓛ 22.00–03.00 Thur & Fri, 22.00–04.00 Sat

The Masquerade One of the city's oldest, liveliest and most popular gay bars attracts punters of all ages and proclivities with cheesy pop, karaoke, cabaret and a friendly vibe. ⓐ 10 Cumberland St ⓣ (0151) 236 7786 ⓛ 11.00–23.00 Sun–Fri, 11.00–01.00 Sat

The Shipping Forecast Fashionable new kid on the nightlife block, this venue brings together art and audio in an array of live events featuring local, national and international talent.

Affordable food is served throughout the day.

ⓐ 15 Slater Street ⓦ www.theshippingforecastliverpool.com

ⓛ 11.00–24.00 Sun–Thur, 11.00–03.00 Fri & Sat

Zanzibar An intimate and often frenetic venue that's popular
with crowds in search of the next 'indie' breakthrough acts.

ⓐ 43 Seel St ⓣ (0151) 707 0633 ⓦ www.thezanzibarclub.com

ⓛ 22.00–03.00 daily

PERFORMANCE ARTS

The Empire Huge venue for national touring shows and
internationally acclaimed acts. ⓐ Lime St ⓣ 0844 847 2525
ⓦ www.liverpoolempire.org.uk

The Liverpool Academy of Arts Intimate theatre showcasing the
work of local stage talent in all its manifestations (see page 80).

ⓐ 36 Seel St ⓣ (0151) 709 9034

The Playhouse This classical theatre often presents fresh
reinterpretations of the old faves. ⓐ Williamson Square
ⓣ (0151) 709 4776 ⓦ www.everymanplayhouse.com

The Royal Court Varied programmes that feature stand-up
comedy, musicals and innovative local dramatic talent.

ⓐ Roe St ⓣ 0870 787 1866 ⓦ www.royalcourtliverpool.com

The Unity Music, dance, song, comedy and new theatrical
works from across the globe grace the stage. ⓐ 1 Hope Place
ⓣ 0844 873 2888 ⓦ www.unitytheatreliverpool.co.uk

The Georgian Quarter

Less than a square kilometre (half a sq mile) in size and lying to the east of the Mersey, the Georgian Quarter sits on a rise that overlooks central Liverpool. It is bordered by the Metropolitan Cathedral to the north and the Anglican Cathedral to the south. Most of the buildings here were constructed for merchants who grew rich during the city's economic heyday. They were built in the style commonly known as 'Georgian', which is characterised by grace, grand decoration and symmetry. The end of that boom saw something of an exodus of the commercial class, which was replaced by an influx of more artistic types who were attracted by the advent of such venues as the Philharmonic Hall (see page 104).

Any fashionable urbanites who don't actually live here come to play and work (but not to shop: there's no retail therapy on offer in this part of town apart from the markets). Students are plentiful, too, as the majority of the city's university buildings are nearby. The fine homes of the businessmen of old are now socialising spots that cater to the needs of today's young, well-off demographic. Although venues here do get busy at weekends and on weekday evenings, the atmosphere is calmer than the high-octane raving that characterises the city centre. During the weekend daylight hours and at the height of summer, the streets empty of traffic and market stalls sell fresh produce, handmade clothing and all other kinds of saleable bohemiana. Residents head to the arty cafés to read chunky newspapers, imbibe large quantities of coffee and plan the night ahead. Wherever they decide to go, buses S1, 1, 25 and 101 will convey them. But it's probably quicker – and certainly more enjoyable – to walk.

⬤ *The futuristic Liverpool Metropolitan Cathedral*

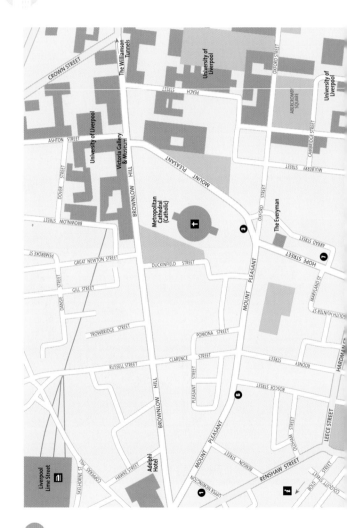

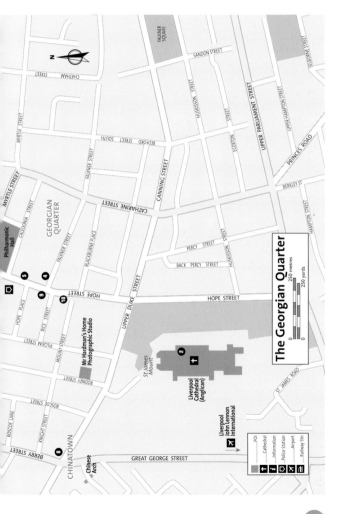

The Georgian Quarter

			POI
	†		Cathedral
	i		Information
			Police Station
	✈		Airport
			Railway Stn

0 ____ 250 metres
0 ____ 250 yards

Philharmonic Hall

GEORGIAN QUARTER

Mr Hardman's Home
Photographic Studio

CHINATOWN

Chinese Arch

St James Mount

Liverpool
Cathedral
(Anglican)

Liverpool
John Lemon
International

○ *The majestic interior of Liverpool Cathedral*

SIGHTS & ATTRACTIONS

Liverpool Cathedral

Liverpool is fortunate to have two very different, but equally stunning, examples of ecclesiastical architecture located at either end of the aptly named Hope Street. Seventy-four years in the making, the Anglican Cathedral wasn't officially completed until 1978 (a decade later than its more modern-looking Catholic near neighbour, see page 96). The competition to win the contract to design the new cathedral was won in 1903 by Giles Gilbert Scott, who, incidentally, also created one of the world's smallest buildings – the iconic red public telephone boxes that were such a feature of Britain's street furniture in the second half of the last century. That's rather ironic given the size of his cathedral, the fifth largest in the world and the largest Anglican cathedral in Europe. The interior is huge, and its aesthetic simplicity and lack of adornment only add to a sense of vastness. A combination of lift and stairs gets you to the top of the tower for some breathtaking views and there is generally a friendly guide waiting to help you should you need information on the sights of the cityscape and surrounding countryside. Directly below, on the eastern side of the cathedral, is the tranquil greenery of a former quarry and graveyard. This is a good place to catch your breath and reflect on this great edifice. The ramps leading down to the old cemetery from street level are said to have been installed to provide easy access for funeral processions and also used to be a place where courting couples could be seen together and even risk a promenade.

ⓐ St James Mount ⓣ (0151) 709 6271

ⓦ www.liverpoolcathedral.org.uk ⓛ 08.00–18.00 daily

Liverpool Metropolitan Cathedral

At the northern extremity of this area is the Catholic cathedral affectionately – though possibly politically incorrectly – known as 'Paddy's Wigwam'. Conforming to a 1960s notion of futurism, it was designed and completed in five years by Sir Frederick Gibberd.

The interior boasts a hugely impressive lantern tower of multicoloured glass that magically bathes the circular knave in a rich blue. The high-vaulted crypt is a must-see as it relates the history of the cathedral and is the only part of the structure designed by Sir Edwin Lutyens in the 1930s that was actually built. The word 'Metropolitan' signifies that the bishop who sits here is the spiritual leader of Catholics across northern England.
ⓐ Mount Pleasant ⓣ (0151) 709 9222
ⓦ www.liverpoolmetrocathedral.org.uk ⓛ 08.00–18.00 daily (summer); 08.00–17.00 daily (winter)

CULTURE

Mr Hardman's Home Photographic Studio

A unique and intimate award-winning museum that charts the life and work of the highly acclaimed photographer Edward Chambré Hardman and his business partner and wife Margaret. As well as being snapper to the stars and a renowned portraitist, Hardman produced beautifully atmospheric landscapes that captured the dramatic changes taking place in the city in the period from the mid-1920s to the mid-1960s. ⓐ 59 Rodney St ⓣ (0151) 709 6261
ⓦ www.nationaltrust.org.uk ⓛ 11.00–15.30 Wed–Sun (Mar–Oct)
ⓘ Admission charge

Victoria Gallery & Museum

Imposing in its red-brick glory on the outside, beautifully tiled on the inside and all thoroughly refurbished, this is an often neglected attraction that displays works of art stretching from the 16th century right up to the present day. Artists featured include Epstein, Turner, Freud and Frink, together with the largest collection of work by American wildlife artist John James Audubon held outside the USA. The museum also hosts exhibits relating to Liverpool University's faculties and their pioneering work in dentistry, archaeology, zoology, engineering and oceanography. 🇦 Ashton St ☎ (0151) 794 2348 🌐 www.liv.ac.uk 🕐 10.00–17.00 Tues–Sat

TAKING A BREAK

Green Fish Café £ ❶ This tucked-away veggie/vegan establishment has been serving the good folk of Merseyside with a wide range of fresh, wholesome and ethically sourced food for nearly 20 years. The award-winning café forms part of the Domino Art Gallery. 🇦 11 Upper Newington ☎ (0151) 707 8592 🌐 www.greenfishcafe.com 🕐 12.00–16.00 Mon–Sat

The Mezzanine Café Bar £ ❷ Relaxing contemporary café that's ideal for a light bite and coffee in the heart of Liverpool Cathedral. It offers wonderful hushed views over stained glass and the Baptistery. Those with pressing business can take advantage of the free Wi-Fi. 🇦 St James Mount ☎ (0151) 709 6271 🌐 www.liverpoolcathedral.org.uk 🕐 09.00–16.30 Mon–Sat, 11.30–14.30 Sun

The Piazza Café £ ❸ Here at the base of the steps leading up to the Metropolitan Cathedral, you can replenish your reserves with coffee, cake and ice cream, or perhaps even partake in a bowl of the local broth, 'Scouse'. ⓐ Mount Pleasant ⓣ (0151) 707 3536 ⓛ 10.00–17.00 daily

The Quarter £ ❹ Laid-back arty café serving a fine choice of teas, coffees and cakes. It has an outside seating area with views over the Anglican Cathedral and offers a selection of breakfast options and quality, Italian-themed food for lunch and dinner. ⓐ 7 Falkner St ⓣ (0151) 707 1965 ⓦ www.thequarteruk.com ⓛ 09.00–23.30 Mon–Fri, 10.00–22.30 Sat & Sun

AFTER DARK

RESTAURANTS
Ego £ ❺ Mediterranean-style dining that scores high on the quality of the carefully sourced produce that makes up its menu's ingredients. Meals are served in a bright and breezy atmosphere next to the Philharmonic Hall. Alfresco eating and drinking is available during the summer months. ⓐ Hope St ⓣ (0151) 706 0707 ⓦ www.egorestaurants.com ⓛ 12.00–22.30 daily

Heart & Soul £ ❻ A cool-toned restaurant with a generally European menu that adds occasional African and Asian influences to the mix. There's a private courtyard for dining or aimlessly whiling away the hours in the full blaze of the British sunshine. ⓐ 62 Mount Pleasant ⓣ (0151) 707 9276 ⓦ www.heartandsoul restaurant.co.uk ⓛ 12.00–23.00 Mon–Sat, 12.00–20.00 Sun

The Side Door Bistro £ ❼ Though resembling an informal
Parisian café in ambience and décor, the continually updated
menu is very much a celebration of British cuisine with many of
its ingredients having only journeyed from just beyond the city
limits. Located close to both the Everyman Theatre and
Philharmonic Hall, pre- and post-dinner specials are available.
ⓐ 29a Hope St ⓣ (0151) 707 7888 ⓦ www.thesidedoor.co.uk
ⓛ 12.00–14.30, 17.30–22.30 Mon–Sat

Yuet Ben £ ❽ This has consistently been one of the most
popular Chinese eateries in the city for the past 40 years.
It's not particularly glamorous, but the authentic cuisine, such

◬ *Ego offers Mediterranean delights*

as aniseed ribs and Peking duck, is legendary. ⓐ 1 Upper Duke St
ⓣ (0151) 709 5772 ⓦ www.yuetben.co.uk ⓛ 17.00–23.00
Tues–Thur, 17.00–24.00 Fri & Sat

The London Carriage Works £££ ⓭ One of Liverpool's leading
restaurants, it is regularly recognised nationally for the quality
of its locally sourced ingredients and the skill with which
they are crafted into classic and contemporary British and
European fare. ⓐ 40 Hope St ⓣ (0151) 705 2222
ⓦ www.thelondoncarriageworks.co.uk ⓛ 12.00–22.00 Mon–Sat,
12.00–21.00 Sun

60 Hope Street £££ ⓾ Quite a formal place – the adjoining bistro
is less so – this multi-award-winning eatery offers a creative,

△ *60 Hope Street – an award-winning institution*

European-influenced menu that's governed to an extent by the seasonality of its ingredients. ⓐ 60 Hope St ⓣ (0151) 707 6060 ⓦ www.60hopestreet.com ⓛ 17.00–22.30 Mon–Sat

PUBS, BARS & CLUBS

Casa A free jukebox and cheap drinks are just two of the reasons why this bar is so popular. It's run by enterprising former dockworkers who took it over after their strike and subsequent job losses in the 1990s, and the fact that many of their ex-colleagues drink here contributes to the atmosphere. Whether you're downstairs in the bistro enjoying cheap food of the steak and curry variety or upstairs in the intimate bar, you'll get a warm welcome. ⓐ 29 Hope St ⓣ (0151) 709 2148 ⓛ 09.30–23.30 Sun–Thur, 09.30–02.00 Fri & Sat

Everyman Bistro The Everyman is a perennially favourite drinking den and cheap, canteen-style food stop among students, actors, media types and the literati. Music and poetry events occur and, come the weekend, the ambience is one of undiluted bonhomie, the chatter convivial. ⓐ 5–9 Hope St ⓣ (0151) 708 9545 ⓦ www.everyman.co.uk ⓛ 12.00–24.00 Sun–Thur, 12.00–02.00 Fri & Sat

Fly in the Loaf Excellent traditional pub that's been in the same family for over 20 years. A good choice of real ale and international beers is one of the draws here, as is the roominess, a large screen for TV sporting events and the extremely friendly staff. ⓐ 13 Hardman St ⓣ (0151) 708 0817 ⓛ 12.00–23.00 Sun–Thur, 12.00–24.00 Fri & Sat

🔺 *The traditional Fly in the Loaf*

Magnet Bar An award-winning bar and live music venue, this destination is ideal for music lovers who want to mix with like-minded souls and listen to some of the grooviest sounds the city has to offer. Upstairs you'll find conversation among the comfy booths, and downstairs gets louder with live international acts and DJs. ⓐ 45 Hardman St ⓣ (0151) 709 7560 ⓦ www.magnetliverpool.co.uk ⓛ 19.00–03.00 Mon–Thur, 19.00–05.00 Fri & Sat

The Philharmonic Dining Rooms Bemoaning his new-found fame, John Lennon once said that the price he had to pay was 'not being able to go to the Phil for a drink'. One can sympathise as this Grade I listed monument to Victorian exuberance is surely one of the most charismatic pubs in Britain. Divided into several rooms, there are enough original period features to keep

THE MOLE OF EDGE HILL

Slightly beyond the western extremity of the Georgian Quarter, following Mount Pleasant past the Metropolitan Cathedral and away from the city centre, is a remarkable attraction hidden among neglected open spaces and a collection of 1960s housing – the Williamson Tunnels. Here, nearly 200 years ago, a certain Joseph Williamson instigated a massive structural project, the purpose of which still confounds people today.

During the 1820s and '30s, builders under Williamson's supervision scratched away at sandstone to create a labyrinth of tunnels and caverns deep beneath the city streets. Although no one can accurately assess the extent of this brick-lined warren (much of it is yet to be revealed), it could well stretch for miles.

Theories as to Williamson's motives abound. Perhaps the most alluring is that he designed the tunnels secretly to connect with the homes of wealthy women. One of the more likely theories is that they were an act of pure philanthropy planned to keep local working men out of the pubs and in paid employment, and to give them a useful apprenticeship for future job seeking. Another persuasive argument is that the tunnels were to be a bolt hole in the event of the Armageddon anticipated by the teachings of his church; Williamson was a deeply religious man and some of the subterranean brickwork architecture does have a resemblance to ecclesiastical styling.

Hopes of gaining any written clues were dashed early on when Williamson's housekeeper sold all his personal papers shortly after his death in 1840. Whatever his purpose, Williamson and his burrowing workers constructed a subterranean marvel. Not only is their achievement a tribute to Victorian ingenuity and dogged determination, but it also makes for a compelling mystery. ⓐ Smithdown Lane ⓣ (0151) 709 6868 ⓦ www.williamsontunnels.co.uk ⓛ 10.00–16.00 Tues–Sun (summer); 10.00–16.00 Thur–Sun (winter) ⓝ Bus: 11 (ask the driver to tell you when to get off) ⓘ Admission charge

you transfixed for hours and even the gents' toilet – which has won awards – is worthy of some study. ⓐ 36 Hope St ⓣ (0151) 707 2837 ⓛ 10.00–23.00 Sun–Thur, 10.00–24.00 Fri & Sat

PERFORMANCE ARTS

The Everyman Home of local writing talent, world premieres and innovative touring work from around the county. ⓐ Hope St ⓣ (0151) 709 4776 ⓦ www.everymanplayhouse.com

Philharmonic Hall Illustrious home of the Royal Liverpool Philharmonic Orchestra and occasional venue for jazz, comedy and classic film showings. ⓐ Hope St ⓣ (0151) 709 3789 ⓦ www.liverpoolphil.com

● *Culture for the masses at the Lady Lever Art Gallery*

OUT OF TOWN
trips

The Wirral

Clearly visible across the River Mersey from Liverpool's waterfront, the Wirral is a large, almost rectangular, peninsula that juts out from the English mainland. On its southern edge, the River Dee separates it from the principality of Wales while its northern edge looks over the Irish Sea. Although close to the city, the Wirral has a distinctive identity of its own. Its principal town, Birkenhead, once a powerhouse of Industrial Revolution productivity, has plenty of fine buildings and streets to admire, including Hamilton Square, where the grand but sadly now redundant Town Hall was deliberately positioned and designed to be a visible fanfare of Birkenhead civic pride to its big-city neighbour across the Mersey. For the neighbouring city-dwellers, the long stretches of uninterrupted sandy coastline offer cliff-top walks, sporting opportunities and tranquil nature reserves. All of this is topped off charmingly by the small seaside resort at New Brighton (see page 110).

GETTING THERE

The Wirral is well served by trains from Liverpool, with a journey time of only ten minutes from Lime Street Station (see page 49) to Birkenhead's Hamilton Square and 30 minutes to the peninsula's extremity at New Brighton. **Mersey Ferries** (ⓣ (0151) 330 1444 ⓦ www.merseyferries.co.uk) offers a direct river crossing from Liverpool's Pier Head. From Castle Street in the city centre, you can take buses 32, 33 or 432 to New Brighton at the northern end of the Wirral, or bus 401 for Birkenhead and

● *Birkenhead's grand Town Hall is at present not in use*

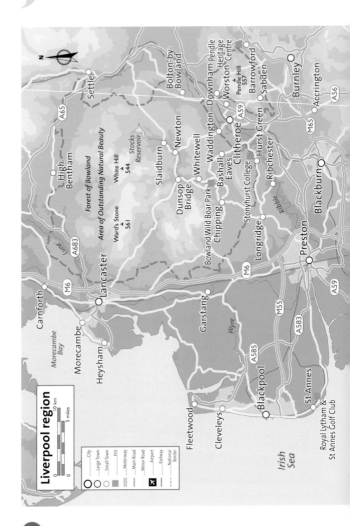

Liverpool region

Legend:
- ◯◯◯ City / Large Town / Small Town
- POI
- Motorway
- Main Road
- Minor Road
- Airport
- Railway
- National Border

0 — 10 km
0 — 5 miles

Irish Sea

Morecambe Bay

Forest of Bowland
Area of Outstanding Natural Beauty

White Hill ▲ 544
Ward's Stone ▲ 561
Pendle Hill ▲ 557

Stocks Reservoir

Ribble
Wyre

Settle
High Bentham
Carnforth
Morecambe
Heysham
Lancaster
Garstang
Fleetwood
Cleveleys
Blackpool
St Annes
Royal Lytham & St Annes Golf Club

Bolton-by-Bowland
Downham
Pendle Heritage Centre
Worston
Barrowford
Sabden
Burnley
Accrington
Slaidburn
Newton
Whitewell
Waddington
Clitheroe
Hurst Green
Dunsop Bridge
Bashall Eaves
Chipping
Stonyhurst College
Ribchester
Longridge
Blackburn
Preston
Bowland Wild Boar Park

Roads: A65, A683, A59, A56, M65, M6, M55, M583, M585, M6

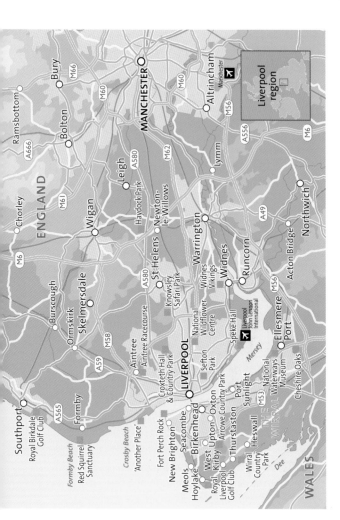

southern destinations. The Wirral is easy to navigate on foot, but public transport details from Liverpool are given for each sight and attraction. To explore by bicycle, contact **Cycle Wirral** (❶ (0151) 336 3938 ❿ www.cyclewirral.co.uk).

SIGHTS & ATTRACTIONS

National Waterways Museum

Cruising on the narrow boats of Britain's canal network has become increasingly popular. This extensive museum set among old canal-side workings traces and re-creates the history of these former industrial highways. ❷ South Pier Rd, Ellesmere Port ❶ (0151) 355 5017 ❿ www.nwm.org.uk ❸ 10.00–17.00 daily ❹ Bus: 1, 11, 401; Train: Ellesmere Port train station, then a ten-minute walk ❶ Admission charge

New Brighton

Although its glory days as a holiday seaside resort have gone, lurid candyfloss and a venerable Art Deco amusement park ensure its popularity. At low tide, a fine, sandy beach reveals itself, overlooked by a promenade and long stretches of well-maintained gardens. A fascinating pointer to local life during wartime is **Fort Perch Rock** (❷ Marine Promenade ❶ 07976 282120 ❸ 12.00–17.00 daily), a historic fortification built in anticipation of a Napoleonic attack. Though the soldiers never fired a shot in justified anger they did once manage to fire twice across the bows of a harmless Norwegian ship. One projectile flew too high and hit the bank on the opposite side of the river; the other pranged an innocent liner. The museum covers military archaeology and the Blitz. Its owner has imaginatively curated a section dedicated to Elvis Presley and local pop heroes. Ⓝ Bus: 10, 10A, 401, 410, 411; Train: New Brighton Station is well served by all Liverpool stations on the Wirral Line

Port Sunlight

This idyllic village was the vision of soap factory magnate Lord William Hesketh Lever, who set himself the target of creating an environment to meet the housing, social, educational and cultural needs of his workers. Deciding to name his little bubble of nirvana after the brand of soap that made him famous (Sunlight), from 1888 he employed no fewer than 30 architects in its design. Lever was keen to include as many European architectural styles as possible, resulting in an eclectic mix of brick, half-timbered and stone-built structures among swathes of parks and gardens. They are still in perfect condition today. All homes were to have proper sanitation (not a common feature in those days), and company profits subsidised village maintenance and financed the construction of a church and college.

It is now a conservation area with 900 Grade II listed buildings spread among its wide open spaces, gardens and pristine, flower-covered dwellings. The compact **Sunlight Vision Museum** (Ⓐ 23 King George's Drive Ⓣ (0151) 644 6466 Ⓦ www.portsunlightvillage.com) tells the story of Lever and his vision for this community, using memorabilia, audiovisual displays and the life stories of the people who lived and worked here. Directly opposite the entrance is the grand classical building of the **Lady Lever Art Gallery** (Ⓐ Queen Mary's Drive Ⓣ (0151) 478 4136 Ⓦ www.liverpoolmuseums.org.uk), which possesses an impressive collection that includes works by artists of the calibre of Millais, Rossetti, Turner and Constable. There are also ceramics, furniture and tapestries. Lever established the gallery so that his workers would have the chance of seeing art up close.

There is a regular rail service between Liverpool Lime Street and Port Sunlight. For details, visit Ⓦ www.merseyrail.org

◉ *The visionary village of Port Sunlight*

Spaceport

State-of-the-art interactive fun for children over seven years of age lurks within six galleries that engagingly tackle life, the universe and everything concerned with space and space travel. There's an impressive 360° planetarium show, while those of a certain vintage will enjoy the retro video games that include many of the old favourites. The museum also hosts special exhibitions and events. ⓐ Seacombe Ferry Terminal ⓣ (0151) 330 1333 ⓦ www.spaceport.org.uk ⓒ 10.30–16.30 Tues–Sun ⓘ Admission charge

U-Boat Story

This new attraction features the German World War II submarine U-534, which saw service as a weather and training vessel. The restored boat has been divided into sections to reveal its inner workings and life on board. Archive films, interactive displays and free guided tours at 14.00 daily tell the tale. ⓐ Woodside Ferry Terminal, Birkenhead ⓣ (0151) 330 1000 ⓦ www.u-boatstory.co.uk ⓒ 10.30–17.00 daily ⓘ Admission charge

Wirral Country Park

An ideal destination for some sea air and gentle exercise. The park centres on a former railway line running parallel to the wild coastal scenery of the River Dee Estuary. The 19 km (12 miles) of now flattened track is relatively gradient free, making it popular with both cyclists and walkers who head here to admire the long stretches of beaches and cliffs and the dramatic views across the water to the mountains of North Wales. There is a visitor centre, a small shop and a café. Guided tours are available. ⓐ Station Rd, Thurstaston ⓣ (0151) 648 4371 ⓦ www.wcpfg.co.uk

RETAIL THERAPY

Cheshire Oaks Located on the southern edge of the Wirral, Cheshire Oaks outlet village is a 140-store shopping extravaganza that retail junkies will find hard to resist – this is where high-street brand names sell off their surplus wares at vastly reduced prices. ⓐ Ellesmere Port ⓣ (0151) 348 5600 ⓦ www.cheshireoaksdesigneroutlet.com ⓛ 10.00–20.00 Mon–Fri, 10.00–19.00 Sat, 10.00–17.00 Sun ⓐ Bus: 1; Train: Ellesmere Port (then 15 minutes to Cheshire Oaks by taxi)

TAKING A BREAK & AFTER DARK

Bridge Inn £ Country-style pub in the heart of Port Sunlight offering food, accommodation and even boasting spirit sightings

GETTING ACTIVE

There are no fewer than 14 golf courses among the Wirral's wide-open spaces, but for those who crave more stimulation, there's high-speed fun such as sand yachting and kitebuggying at Meols and Hoylake beaches (ⓦ www.wsyc.org.uk). For sailing and windsurfing go to **West Kirby Marine Centre** (ⓐ Sandy Lane, West Kirby ⓣ (0151) 625 5579 ⓦ www.wksc.net). Equine adventures, including hacks along the beaches, are available from **Park Lane Liveries** (ⓐ East View Farm, Park Rd, Meols ⓣ (0151) 632 0839 ⓦ www.parklaneliveries.co.uk).

of the paranormal kind. ⓐ Bolton Rd, Port Sunlight ⓣ (0151) 645 8441 ⓦ www.goodnightinns.co.uk ⓛ 12.00–24.00 daily

The Wro £ This multi-award-winning wine bar and restaurant attracts sophisticates from near and far. Along with British and international menu staples served throughout the day, a selection of grazing menus is available to share. ⓐ Grange Rd, West Kirby ⓣ (0151) 625 2010 ⓦ www.thewro-lounge.co.uk ⓛ 10.00–21.30 (food) Tues–Sun

Sheldrakes £–££ With captivating views across the Dee Estuary and Welsh mountains beyond, this is an excellent stop for a Mediterranean-influenced lunch or dinner or even just a refreshing drink. ⓐ Banks Rd, Lower Heswall ⓣ (0151) 342 1556 ⓦ www.sheldrakesrestaurant.co.uk ⓛ 11.00–24.00 daily

Fraiche £££ Award-winning modern French cuisine is served for lunch or dinner. Choose from a selection of set tasting menus. Reservation is a must. ⓐ 11 Rose Mount, Oxton ⓣ (0151) 652 2914 ⓦ www.restaurantfraiche.com ⓛ 12.00–13.30 until end of lunch, 19.00–20.00 until end of dinner Wed–Sun

ACCOMMODATION

The Wirral is easily and quickly accessible from Liverpool. If you prefer to stay on this side of the water, contact **Visit Wirral** (ⓣ (0151) 666 3188 ⓦ www.visitwirral.com) for advice on somewhere to stay.

The Ribble Valley

Everyone has heard of the dramatic mountain landscapes of northern Wales and the majesty and beauty of the English Lake District. But here is a hidden gem of a place that's changed little over the centuries. The Ribble Valley is a stunningly beautiful area of countryside in northern Lancashire. Its vast, untamed moorland is carpeted by purple and yellow heather and looks over valleys of lush pasture that are criss-crossed by drystone walls. Here are small, solidly built ancient villages and tiny market towns that retain their independent shops, ancient abbeys, castles, myths and folklore. Within the valley, the Forest of Bowland, a designated Area of Outstanding Natural Beauty, adds to the loveliness and hosts a number of protected flora and fauna species.

⬤ *Beyond the untamed countryside, Pendle Hill broods*

Few visitors venture this way, so roads and trails are amazingly clear of traffic and there's no sense whatsoever that eliciting cash from tourists at any cost is the principal preoccupation of the people who run the local attractions, shops or hotels.

GETTING THERE

The journey to the Ribble Valley using public transport is no longer or more complicated than that to North Wales or the Lake District. While there are no direct train routes from Liverpool Lime Street Station, one change is all you need: take the Liverpool to Manchester Victoria service and change trains there for the direct hourly service to Clitheroe (details are available via ❶ 08457 484950 ❿ www.nationalrail.co.uk). If you decide to go by car, follow the signs out of the city centre for the M58 or

M62. Take these to the M6 and head north to Preston, where you take the exit at junction 31 for the A59 to Clitheroe, at the heart of the Ribble Valley.

Pendle Tourist Information Office  Pendle Heritage Centre, Barrowford  (01282) 677150  www.visitpendle.com  10.00–17.00 daily

Ribble Valley Tourist Information Office  Ribble Valley Borough Council Offices, Church Walk, Clitheroe  (01200) 425566  09.00–17.00 Mon–Sat

SIGHTS & ATTRACTIONS

Bowland Wild Boar Park

This small petting zoo features wild boars and an assortment of other unlikely Lancashire animals, plus a selection of short trails through woodland. There is a café and shop that sells a choice of pre-packed wild boar cuts.  On the Chipping to Dunsop Bridge road  (01995) 61554  www.wildboarpark.co.uk  10.30–17.00 daily  Admission charge

Pendle Heritage Centre

Housed in a former farmhouse, this is a gentle and informative museum dedicated to telling the tale of local life during the 17th century, including the infamous Pendle witch trials. There is a shop, local information centre and tea room offering some choice sticky buns and a selection of Lancashire fare.  Park Hill, Barrowford  (01282) 677150  www.htnw.co.uk  11.00–16.00 daily  Bus: 10, 11, P70, P71  Admission charge

Pendle Hill

The valley's highest point – it peaks at 557 m (1,827 ft) – is a magnet for walkers, fell runners and hang-gliders. Pendle Hill is linked with two events that sit at either end of the spiritual spectrum: one concerns witchcraft in the early 1600s and the eventual execution of local women and their families; in the same century, George Fox was drawn to this hill by what he interpreted as a divine force and, on seeing the spectacular views across northern England, Wales and southern Scotland, was inspired to create the Quaker Movement. The Pendle Way is a walking trail that sweeps around the hill along an attractive 72-km (45-mile) footpath. ⓥ Bus: 21, 22, 23, P70, P71

Ribchester

This peaceful, gorgeous village was once home to a Roman fort and was a garrison town that accommodated a thriving military and civilian community. While most of the site has

🔺 *Explore the museum at Pendle Heritage Centre*

THE REAL-LIFE MIDDLE EARTH

Deep in the heart of 1940s Lancashire, a tale unfolded. Following his success with *The Hobbit*, J R R Tolkien was spending a great deal of his time at Stonyhurst College (see below), a Jesuit boarding school where he occasionally taught and to which he had entrusted the education of his son. Here he began his sequel, *The Lord of the Rings*, drawing inspiration from the atmospheric rural surroundings to create its location, 'Middle Earth'. The local village of Hurst Green became Hobbiton, home of Frodo Baggins; the River Shirbourn was modelled on the River Ribble. The sometimes sinister demeanour of brooding Pendle Hill inspired the Misty Mountains.

Today, a 9-km (5½-mile) circular walk has been devised to trace these points of interest (phone ☎ (01200) 425566 for details). The route passes the **Shireburn Arms Hotel** (ⓐ Whalley Rd, Hurst Green ☎ (01254) 826518 ⓦ www.shireburnarmshotel.com), where Tolkien was said to have spent many a happy hour.

been covered, there are the remnants of a bathhouse and an informative museum to explore. ☎ (01254) 878261 ⓦ www.ribchestermuseum.org ⓝ Bus: 3, 5

Stonyhurst College

Magnificent from the outside, breathtaking on the inside, this 16th-century school has hosted a number of celebrities. During the English Civil War Oliver Cromwell slept here before the decisive battle at nearby Preston; Arthur Conan Doyle studied here, as did *The Lord of the Rings* author J R R Tolkien (see opposite). The college is also home to a number of historical artefacts, including the book carried by Mary, Queen of Scots to her execution. ☎ (01254) 826345 ⏱ 13.00–16.30 Sat–Thur (July & Aug) 🚌 Bus: 5 ❶ Admission charge

Valley villages

Dotted across the area, these rural communities have changed little over the centuries and have certainly never succumbed to commercialised excesses. Just about every village is a picture-postcard location – Chipping, Downham, Waddington, Newton, Bolton-by-Bowland and Slaidburn – and all make excellent bases or pit stops when you are exploring this region.

RETAIL THERAPY

Clitheroe, the principal town in the area, offers a wealth of fine shopping including **The Coffee Exchange** (ⓐ Wellgate ☎ (01200) 442270) for all your caffeine needs. You may not associate the word 'Ribble' with oenophilia, but **Byrne & Sons** (ⓐ King St ☎ (01200) 423152 🌐 www.dbyrne-finewines.co.uk) is regarded as one of the best stops for wine and spirits in the country. Self-caterers might want to head for **Cowman's** (ⓐ Castle St ☎ (01200) 423842) for their vast and creative array of sausages. Just outside the town, **Bashall Barn** (ⓐ Twitter Lane ☎ (01200) 428964 🌐 www.bashallbarn.co.uk) features a range of spectacular local produce and quirky gifts. Nearby **Backridge Barn**

(ⓐ Twitter Lane, Waddington ⓦ www.backridge.co.uk) finds space for the works of local artistic talent among its various galleries.

TAKING A BREAK & AFTER DARK

The Emporium £ A stylish café-brasserie in the area's largest town, Clitheroe, that serves coffee, light bites and fine Mediterranean food. An extensive wine list adds to the appeal. ⓐ Moor Lane, Clitheroe ⓣ (01200) 444174 ⓦ www.theemporiumclitheroe.co.uk ⓛ 09.30–23.00 Mon–Sat, 10.30–16.30 Sun

Puddle Ducks £ Old-fashioned tea shop situated in the closest community to the official geographic centre of the United Kingdom. ⓐ Dunsop Bridge ⓣ (01200) 448241 ⓦ www.puddleduckstearooms.co.uk ⓛ 09.30–16.30 Tues–Sun

The Red Pump £–££ Traditional inn with open fires, extensive real ales and wines and some of the best steaks in the area. It also offers overnight accommodation. ⓐ Clitheroe Rd, Bashall Eaves ⓣ (01254) 826227 ⓦ www.theredpumpinn.co.uk ⓛ 12.00–14.30, 18.00–23.00 Tues–Sat, 12.00–21.00 Sun

The Black Bull ££ Rustic food served with passion, flair and a smile, the traditional British pub exterior and location belies the French magic taking place inside this highly regarded bistro and bar. ⓐ Rimington Lane, Rimington ⓣ (01200) 415960 ⓦ www.theblackbullrimington.com ⓛ 12.00–14.30, 18.00–20.45 daily (food)

GETTING ACTIVE

The sheer outdoor magnificence of the Ribble Valley would transform the most inert couch potato into an exercise-obsessed dynamo, and there's no shortage of things to do and organisations set up to help you do them.

Cycle Adventure (① 07518 373007 ⓦ www.cycle-adventure.co.uk) and **Off the Rails** (① (01729) 824419 ⓦ www.offtherails.org.uk) will get you on your bike, and if you fancy the contemplative pursuit of fishing, contact **Fishing Stocks Reservoir** (① (01200) 446602 ⓦ www.stocksreservoir.com) or **Pendle View Fisheries** (① (01200) 822208 ⓦ www.pendleviewfishery.com). Equine-based exercise is on offer at **Braeden Pony Trekking Centre** (ⓦ www.braedens.co.uk), and you can go up, up and away courtesy of both **Bowland Forest Gliding Club** (ⓦ www.bfgc.co.uk) and the **Pendle Balloon Company** (① (01254) 247014 ⓦ www.pendle-balloon-flights.co.uk). You can't go on the piste here, but you can try some dry-slope skiing at **Pendle Ski Club** (① (01200) 425222 ⓦ www.pendleskiclub.org).

ACCOMMODATION

LODGINGS

Angram Green Farmhouse £ Stunningly located B & B accommodation within a working farm at the foot of Pendle Hill. It's equipped to cater for walkers and cyclists. ⓐ Worston ① (01200) 441 441 ⓦ www.angramgreenfarm.co.uk

Calf's Head £ Extremely popular watering hole in the hamlet of Worston offering some fine food, great views and individually designed rooms within a building dating from the 17th century. ⓐ Worston ⓘ (01200) 441218 ⓦ www.calfshead.co.uk

The Inn at Whitewell ££ Former hunting lodge that's popular with the country set, media types and locals. The hospitality is peerless, the food fantastic, the bedrooms eccentric. ⓐ Whitewell ⓘ (01200) 448222 ⓦ www.innatwhitewell.com

The Gibbon Bridge ££–£££ Award-winning hotel surrounded by manicured gardens and its own helicopter pad. Attracting celebrities, this paean to luxury is famous for the creativity of its menu and the sumptuous, well-equipped suites and rooms. ⓐ Green Lane, Chipping ⓘ (01995) 61456 ⓦ www.gibbon-bridge.co.uk

CAMPSITES
Chipping Camping Barn ⓐ Clarkhouse Farm, Chipping ⓘ (01629) 592700
Clitheroe Camping and Caravanning Club Site ⓐ Edisford Rd, Clitheroe ⓘ (01200) 425294
Cross Lanes Caravan & Camping Park ⓐ Cross Lane, Waddington ⓘ (01200) 423568 ⓦ www.crosslanecaravans.co.uk

---

❍ *Sightseeing buses are a good way to see the city*

PRACTICAL
information

Directory

GETTING THERE

By air

Liverpool's John Lennon International Airport (see page 48) has come on in leaps and bounds over the past few years and is now connected to some 60 destinations across Europe. It is a major hub for low-cost carriers such as **easyJet** (Ⓦ www.easyjet.com) and **Ryanair** (Ⓦ www.ryanair.com). For those travelling from further afield, **Manchester Airport** (Ⓦ www.manchesterairport.co.uk), an hour away by road, has a larger choice of international and long-haul services, is well served from North America and has up to 40 flights a day making the 40-minute journey to (and from) London.

Many people are aware that air travel emits CO_2, which contributes to climate change. You may be interested in the possibility of lessening the environmental impact of your flight through the charity **Climate Care** (Ⓦ www.jpmorganclimatecare.com), which offsets your CO_2 by funding environmental projects around the world.

By rail

Virgin Trains operate an hourly high-speed rail link between London's Euston Station and Liverpool Lime Street. It takes approximately two-and-a-half hours. Services from other UK cities, including Manchester Airport (see above), are operated by a variety of different companies.

National Rail Ⓦ www.nationalrail.co.uk
Virgin Trains Ⓦ www.virgintrains.co.uk

By road

National Express coaches run daily routes between all of Britain's major towns and cities, including an eight-times-a-day service from London's Victoria to Liverpool that takes on average six hours, depending on the traffic and time of day. Budget operator Megabus also connects Liverpool with London and Birmingham.

Megabus ☎ 0900 160 0900 Ⓦ www.megabus.com
National Express ☎ 0871 781 8178 Ⓦ www.nationalexpress.com

▲ *The iconic Liverpool Lime Street*

Those travelling from the north or south of the country by car will more than likely use the M6 motorway and then take one of the M62, M58, M56 (and M53) motorways into the city centre. Those travelling from the east will cross the country using the M62. Both the AA and RAC offer free downloadable route maps from their sites.

AA Ⓦ www.theaa.com

RAC Ⓦ www.rac.co.uk

ENTRY FORMALITIES

Passport holders of the EU, Republic of Ireland, USA, Canada, Australia, New Zealand and South Africa need only a valid passport to enter the UK, provided the stay is for no longer than six months. Those travelling from other countries should either consult the British Embassy in their own country or visit the easy-to-follow Ⓦ www.ukvisas.gov.uk for details on visa requirements.

MONEY

Despite pressures from home and abroad to convert to the euro, the official currency of Great Britain is still the pound, which is denoted by the £ sign. One pound equals 100 pence and cash is supplied in the following denominations: notes are available in £50, £20, £10 and £5, while coinage comes in £2, £1 and 50, 20, 10, 5, 2 and 1 pence pieces (also known as simply 'p'). If you arrive having previously travelled in Scotland, the Isle of Man or Northern Ireland, you may have collected some of their differently designed currency. While this is legal tender throughout the UK, smaller shopkeepers may be reluctant to take it in England and it's generally best policy to try to change it to English designs before arriving. More importantly, non-English UK currency can also be viewed with deep suspicion when trying to exchange money abroad.

There are plenty of 24-hour ATM machines (known locally as cashpoints or 'holes in the wall') located outside banks and scattered throughout the city, though some at the airport, main railway stations, retail centres and even in bars may charge a fee for use. Visa and MasterCard are accepted just about everywhere, though American Express cardholders may be limited to upmarket large hotels, shops and restaurants. Anyone wanting to exchange traveller's cheques and foreign currency can visit banks, bureaux de change and larger travel agents (please note that you will be asked to produce a passport to complete the exchange process).

HEALTH, SAFETY & CRIME

Other than over-indulgence, there are no health issues with food and drink in the UK. Although bottled water is freely available, water direct from the tap is safe to drink and more eco-friendly.

The National Health Service (NHS) entitles British and EU citizens to free medical treatment, though anyone visiting from outside will find they have to pay for treatment. If you live outside the European Union, adequate health insurance must be arranged before travelling. Pharmacists (chemists) are happy to diagnose and prescribe help for most minor conditions and you can also pick up mild painkillers and cough and cold remedies from supermarkets and small shops. Those on a course of prescription drugs will need to carry paperwork such as the prescription or letter from your doctor when entering the country.

Like all major cities throughout the world, Liverpool has its fair share of criminals and ne'er-do-wells and areas best avoided, particularly late at night (though these tend to be the areas outside of the city centre). The rule of thumb should always be that if your instincts tell you not go somewhere, then your instincts are probably right. Whatever time of day, keep a firm grip on bags and cameras, with wallets and purses stowed in inside pockets. Uniformed police keep a high profile in the busier areas during the day and night. In general, they are a friendly, approachable bunch and should be informed of any incident straight away.

OPENING HOURS

Shops generally open 09.00 to 17.30 Monday to Saturday. Some stores open until 19.00 or 20.00 during the week and for a few hours on a Sunday. Most will be open on bank and public holidays (see page 11). Banks are open 09.30 to 16.30 Monday to Friday. More and more banks also open on Saturdays, though all close on bank holidays, which generally fall on a Monday. Cash is available 365 days a year from ATMs.

TOILETS

Galleries, museums and large department stores all have well-maintained toilet facilities. There are also a number of public conveniences dotted around the city, though standards of quality can be inconsistent and a small fee is often required. Should none of these be available, pubs and bars will be able to help out, though it is customary to buy a drink first or at least politely ask the person serving if you can use the facilities.

CHILDREN

Although the 'children should be seen and not heard' attitude of the British towards youngsters is all but extinct these days, certain eating and drinking establishments will still put a poster on the wall directing parents as to the required behaviour of their cherished ones. Generally, though, children whose deportment stays on the right side of anarchic are welcomed in most places. Happily, the 2007 ban on smoking in public places has meant that a lot more places are healthy and friendly environments in which to take little ones, and many eating establishments offer special kid's menus. Baby food, nappies and any other accessories can be purchased from supermarkets and high-street stores such as Boots and Superdrug.

Children's attractions in and around the city include the fabulous science-and-art discovery centre of **Underwater Street** on Water Street (ⓣ (0151) 227 2550 ⓦ www.underwaterstreet.com). **Knowsley Safari Park** (ⓣ (0151) 430 9009 ⓦ www.knowsley.com) offers roaming wild and exotic animals that can be viewed from the safety of your car on the eastern edge of the city. For those interested in an up-close encounter with creepy-crawlies, **Bug World Experience** should also prove a winner (ⓐ Albert Dock ⓦ www.bugworldexperience.co.uk ⓛ 10.00–16.00 daily ⓘ Admission charge).

COMMUNICATIONS

Internet

You'll never be too far from access to the web and Internet in Liverpool, with many bars and cafés now featuring wireless connectivity as one of their attractions. Most hotels also offer access, though some may charge you for the privilege. Le Boulevard has pay-as-you-go Internet cafés in both Clayton Square and Lewis's department store on Ranelagh Street.

Phone

Although the classic red phone boxes are now noticeable by their absence, there are still payphones available inside attractions, museums, bars and restaurants that accept either cash or credit cards. A number of UK mobile phone providers will announce their service via your handset on arrival in the UK. Coverage throughout Liverpool is generally very good.

UK Operator number 🛈 100
International Operator 🛈 155

TELEPHONING GREAT BRITAIN

To telephone Liverpool from outside the United Kingdom, dial the international code (011 from North America, 0011 from Australia, 00 from New Zealand) plus the country code (44) plus 151 followed by the individual number.

TELEPHONING ABROAD

To telephone abroad from the UK, dial 00 followed by the relevant country code, then the area code (minus the first zero) and local number.

Australia 61	New Zealand 64
Canada 1	South Africa 27
Eire 353	USA 1

Post

The postal service in the UK is still regarded as one of the best in the world in terms of reliability and speed, and a first-class stamp will generally get a letter to a UK destination on the following day if posted during normal office hours. Mail sent to mainland Europe usually takes three or four days depending upon the local service of its destination, while mail going further afield can take between seven and ten days. Liverpool's central post office is within the Liverpool ONE shopping centre (W H Smith's second floor) and is open from Monday to Saturday (09.00–17.00). Other post office sub-branches close at noon on Saturdays. Stamps for letters and postcards can be bought from most general stores, gift and card shops and should be posted into the traditional red free-standing circular or wall-mounted postboxes.

ELECTRICITY

British electrical voltage is 240V, supplied through a three-pinned plug. Most overseas visitors will need only a plug adaptor (available in your home country), though some equipment may also need a transformer if it runs on 110V.

TRAVELLERS WITH DISABILITIES

Liverpool is not a particularly hilly city, though the terrain does gently rise as it passes through the centre away from the River Mersey. Virtually all museums, galleries and other attractions will have made some provision for easy wheelchair access, although older buildings that house pubs, bars and restaurants may be restricted by both structure and protected heritage status. Public transport is wheelchair-friendly, as are many of the newer black taxis. **DisabledGo** (ⓦ www.disabledgo.info) and **Holiday Care** (ⓣ 0845 124 9971 ⓦ www.holidaycare.org.uk) provide information on access and transport to many of the city's venues. **Shopmobility** (ⓐ 35 Strand St ⓣ (0151) 707 0877 ⓦ www.localsolutions.org.uk) can hire electric scooters and other transport for periods ranging from a few hours to a few days.

TOURIST INFORMATION

There are three tourist information points in Liverpool. The largest and most comprehensive is in the city centre and offers an array of books, maps and leaflets covering all of the events and attractions in the city. The enthusiastic and friendly staff can offer advice on eating and drinking, travel and day trips as well as help with accommodation and theatre bookings. The two other offices are located at Albert Dock on the Waterfront and Liverpool John Lennon Airport.

Albert Dock Visitor Information Centre ⓐ Anchor Courtyard, Albert Dock ⓣ (0151) 233 2008 ⓛ 10.00–17.00 daily

City Centre Tourist Information Centre ⓐ Whitechapel ⓣ (0151) 233 2008 ⓛ 09.00–18.00 Mon–Sat, 11.00–16.00 Sun

Liverpool John Lennon Airport Tourist Information Desk ⓐ Arrivals Hall ⓣ (0151) 233 2008 ⓛ 07.00–20.00 daily

The following websites are also useful sources of information:

ⓦ www.liverpool.com

ⓦ www.visitliverpool.com

ⓦ www.visitnorthwest.com

BACKGROUND READING

2008 Reasons Why Merseyside is the Capital of Football
by John Keith and Gavin Buckland. The triumphs, tears and
humour inspired by Merseyside's three clubs.

Liverpool 800: Culture, Character and History edited by
John Belchem. Warts-and-all portrait of the city and its
people by a selection of local experts.

Liverpool Through the Lens by Mike McCartney and Edward
Chambré Hardman. The city captured between the 1920s and
1970s by two famous local photographers.

*Liverpool – Wondrous Place: From the Cavern to the Capital
of Culture* by Paul Du Noyer. Study of the wealth of musical
talent from the city.

The Mersey Sound by Adrian Henri, Roger McGough and Brian
Patten. An introduction to contemporary poetry by three of the
city's greats.

More Than Just a Hairdresser by Nia Pritchard. Bubbly local
hairdressing talent turns to private investigation.

The Story of Liverpool by Alex Tulloch. Popular history of the city
without academic facts and figures.

Twopence to Cross the Mersey by Helen Forrester. A story
of family life in the slums of 1930s Liverpool.

Emergencies

EMERGENCY NUMBERS
For police, fire or ambulance services call ⓘ 999

MEDICAL SERVICES
Late-night pharmacy
Tesco ⓐ St Oswald St, Old Swan ⓘ 0845 677 9523 ⓛ 08.00–22.30
Mon–Sat, 10.00–16.00 Sun. Alternative pharmacies can be
located by looking at the list on any pharmacy door.

Hospitals
The Royal Liverpool University Hospital Centrally located hospital
offering an accident and emergency department 24 hours a day.
ⓐ Prescot St ⓘ (0151) 706 2000
NHS Walk-In Centre For minor ailments such as skin conditions,
cuts, strains, sprains and stomach problems. ⓐ 53 Great
Charlotte St ⓘ (0151) 285 3535 ⓛ 07.00–22.00 Mon–Fri,
09.00–22.00 Sat & Sun

Doctors
If you need medical advice, **NHS Direct** (ⓘ 0845 4647) operates a
24-hour-a-day service offering professional advice on symptoms
and medical conditions. If necessary, they will make you an
appointment to see a doctor at the earliest possible time.

Dentists
Liverpool University Dental Hospital (ⓐ Pembroke Place
ⓘ (0151) 706 5060 ⓛ 08.00–17.00 daily) offers an accident and

emergency department for severe dental problems only and operates on a first-come, first-served basis.

POLICE

The police should be contacted in an emergency by calling ☎ 999. Officers patrol the streets 'on the beat' along with Community Support Officers, and while the latter do not have the same powers as the police, they are a good source of advice and help and can react positively and effectively if any misdemeanours have taken place. Also scattered around the city centre are a number of help points which offer intercom connections to local operators, who are there to help if you're feeling in any way threatened.

Police HQ The Waterfront offices of the Merseyside Police service are close to the city centre and are open 24 hours a day. ⓐ Canning Place ☎ (0151) 709 6010

EMBASSIES & CONSULATES

Australian High Commission ⓐ Australia House, Strand, London ☎ (020) 7379 4334 ⓦ www.australia.org.uk

Canadian High Commission ⓐ 1 Grosvenor Square, London ☎ (020) 7258 6600 ⓦ www.canada.org.uk

Irish Embassy ⓐ 17 Grosvenor Place, London ☎ (020) 7235 2171 ⓦ www.ireland.embassyhomepage.com

New Zealand High Commission ⓐ New Zealand House, 80 Haymarket, London ☎ (020) 7930 8422 ⓦ www.nzembassy.com

South African High Commission ⓐ South Africa House, Trafalgar Square, London ☎ (020) 7451 7299 ⓦ www.southafricahouse.com

US Embassy ⓐ 24 Grosvenor Square, London ☎ (020) 7499 9000 ⓦ www.usembassy.org.uk

ACKNOWLEDGEMENTS

The publishers would like to thank the following individuals and organisations for supplying their copyright photographs for this book: Beatles Story/The Mersey Partnership, page 13; David Cawley, page 127; Dreamstime.com (Stephen Mcnally, page 5; Jmci, pages 116–17; Andrew Tunney, page 119; Debu55x, page 125); flickr.com (thinboyfatter, page 47; Gene Hunt, page 86); iStockphoto (Chris Hepurn, page 23; Joe Clemson, page 57); Malmaison, pages 35 & 70; Peter Owen/Sefton Tourism, page 16; Redvers, page 48; Wendy Slattery, pages 45, 59, 64, 69, 75, 99, 100 & 102; sxc.hu (Kalervo Kekkonen, page 94); Wikimedia Commons (Boing! said Zebedee, page 15; Chowells, pages 40–41); World Pictures/Photoshot, pages 29 & 72; The Mersey Partnership, all others.

Project editor: Rosalind Munro
Layout: Trevor Double
Proofreaders: Cath Senker & Karolin Thomas

Send your thoughts to
books@thomascook.com

- Found a great bar, club, shop or must-see sight that we don't feature?
- Like to tip us off about any information that needs a little updating?
- Want to tell us what you love about this handy little guidebook and more importantly how we can make it even handier?

Then here's your chance to tell all! Send us ideas, discoveries and recommendations today and then look out for your valuable input in the next edition of this title.

Email the above address (stating the title) or write to:
pocket guides Series Editor, Thomas Cook Publishing, PO Box 227, Coningsby Road, Peterborough PE3 8SB, UK.

WHAT'S IN YOUR GUIDEBOOK?

Independent authors Impartial up-to-date information from our travel experts who meticulously source local knowledge.

Experience Thomas Cook's 165 years in the travel industry and guidebook publishing enriches every word with expertise you can trust.

Travel know-how Thomas Cook has thousands of staff working around the globe, all living and breathing travel.

Editors Travel-publishing professionals, pulling everything together to craft a perfect blend of words, pictures, maps and design.

You, the traveller We deliver a practical, no-nonsense approach to information, geared to how you really use it.

ABOUT THE AUTHOR

A member of The British Guild of Travel Writers and published throughout the world, David Cawley is a freelance travel and history writer and radio broadcaster based in the northwest of England. David is a history graduate of Liverpool University and remains a regular visitor to the city in a professional, cultural and hedonistic capacity.

shed
nds,
avel.

s our
crets
orld,
th of
ravel

yo
t trip
tage.

Thomas Cook pocket guides

PARIS

Your travelling companion since 1873

Thomas
Cook

Thomas Cook **pocket** guides

PARIS

Your travelling companion since 1873

Thomas Cook